The Complete Acid Reflux Cookbook

A Lot of Flavorful Recipes and a 28-Day Meal Plan to Conquer GERD & LPR with Fluency and Ease | Embrace Comfort, Banish Discomfort, and Savor Every Bite

Sara Creighton

TABLE OF CONTENTS

INTRODUCTION

Welcome to a journey of flavor, health, and happiness. This path centers around a common yet often misunderstood condition, acid reflux, which, when left unchecked, can lead to more severe conditions such as gastroesophageal reflux disease (GERD) and laryngopharyngeal reflux (LPR).

But don't worry, you're not alone on this adventure. As a fellow traveler who understands the discomfort and distress these conditions can cause, the aim is to help you navigate this journey with a resource beyond a conventional cookbook. The objective? To empower you to conquer GERD and LPR through the incredible power of food.

Food is more than just sustenance. It's a celebration of culture, a pillar of health, and a vessel of joy. Yet, food can seem like a double-edged sword for those suffering from acid reflux. This doesn't have to be your reality. You deserve to savor each meal, look forward to your lunch break, and delight in dinner preparations. You deserve to enjoy food without fear or discomfort.

That's where this comprehensive acid reflux cookbook comes into play. Crafted with care and understanding, it's loaded with flavorful recipes that are both delicious and gentle on your digestive system. These recipes focus on fresh, whole foods and nutrient-rich ingredients and are tailored to soothe your stomach, reduce inflammation, and keep those pesky reflux symptoms at bay.

But the book goes beyond simply providing recipes. It's a comprehensive guide and an ally that walks with you step by step, meal by meal, as you make simple yet impactful dietary changes. Embedded in its pages is a specially designed 28-day meal plan. This plan is more than just a menu; it's a transformative tool that helps you reclaim control over your health and well-being.

The 28-day meal plan doesn't just tell you what to eat. It provides structure, variation, and balance, ensuring that you're nourished and satisfied without aggravating your reflux symptoms. Each day's menu is carefully crafted to provide balanced nutrition, taking into account the right mix of protein, carbohydrates, and fats, along with ample fruits and vegetables.

And there's more. The portion sizes and meal timings have been thoughtfully planned to optimize your digestion and prevent common reflux triggers. From the moment you start your day with a soothing breakfast to the comfort of a light yet satisfying dinner, this meal plan paves the way for a new, positive relationship with food.

Remember, change is a process, not an event. It's about taking small, steady steps toward your health goals. You're making progress with each recipe you try and each meal you enjoy. You're not just managing your symptoms but also working towards long-term health, all while delighting in delicious food.

In the following pages, you'll find an array of dishes bursting with flavor and nutrition. You'll discover that a diet for GERD and LPR doesn't mean deprivation or blandness. On the contrary, it's an opportunity to explore, experiment, and enjoy. It's an invitation to relish every bite without worry, embrace comfort, and banish discomfort.

So, turn the page on acid reflux and say hello to a world where you can truly savor every bite because you deserve nothing less.

Navigating life with acid reflux, GERD, or LPR can often seem challenging, particularly regarding food choices. However, understanding your diet's critical role in managing these conditions can illuminate the path to relief and overall wellness. Let's delve into why food matters so much when living with acid reflux and its more severe counterparts, GERD and LPR.

The food you consume profoundly impacts your health, and this impact magnifies when dealing with acid reflux. Picture your stomach as a small bag that's supposed to handle acid, much like a battery that holds electricity. Your stomach lining is built to withstand this acid, but your esophagus isn't. When you eat foods that trigger your acid reflux, your stomach produces more acid. This excess acid can backflow into your esophagus, causing the burning sensation commonly known as heartburn, one of the hallmarks of acid reflux.

So, how does diet come into play? Well, some foods are known to increase stomach acid and relax the lower esophageal sphincter, the muscle connecting your esophagus to your stomach. When this muscle relaxes at the wrong times, it allows the acidic contents of your stomach to backflow into your esophagus, leading to acid reflux symptoms.

That's where the power of an appropriately tailored diet shines. A diet that helps manage acid reflux is all about balance and making mindful choices. It involves including foods that are easy on your stomach and avoiding foods that can potentially trigger reflux symptoms.

Contrary to popular belief, a diet that manages acid reflux, GERD, or LPR doesn't have to be restrictive or bland. It simply involves understanding your triggers, finding suitable alternatives, and learning how to combine foods to minimize discomfort. For instance, swapping highly acidic fruits like oranges with low-acid fruits like bananas can improve your digestive comfort. Choosing lean proteins and whole grains over fatty foods and refined carbs can reduce the likelihood of triggering acid reflux.

Moreover, a well-managed diet doesn't just help reduce reflux symptoms; it can also promote overall health and well-being. It can help you maintain a healthy weight, a crucial factor in managing acid reflux, as excess weight puts additional pressure on your stomach, increasing the risk of acid backflow.

And it doesn't stop there. Eating a balanced, nutrient-rich diet boosts your immunity, promotes gut health, enhances mood, and fuels your body with the energy you need to lead an active, fulfilling life.

The secret is to embrace this path with an open mind. Explore new flavors, experiment with different cooking methods, and discover the joy of creating meals that not only taste fantastic but also feel good to your body.

Each body is unique, and what works for one may not work for another. Therefore, the goal isn't to find a one-size-fits-all solution but to understand your body, listen to its signals, and respond with love and care.

The hope is to help you turn mealtime from a source of stress into a source of joy and healing. From this point forward, your journey will nourish your body, calm your digestive system, and reclaim the joy of eating.

When we think of diet, we often focus on what we should or shouldn't eat or how much we should or shouldn't consume. While these factors are undeniably important, there's another aspect of eating that's just as critical to our overall well-being yet frequently overlooked – the straightforward enjoyment of food.

Yes, believe it or not, taking pleasure in what you eat is an essential part of a healthy lifestyle. Food is not merely a source of nutrients; it's a source of joy, comfort, and fulfillment. It's an integral part of our social lives, our cultural identities, and our personal narratives. Therefore, when you enjoy your food, you're nurturing not just your body but also your soul.

You may think, "How can I enjoy my food when I have to avoid so many things because of acid reflux?" That's a legitimate concern. But here's the thing: a diet that helps manage acid reflux doesn't have to be a diet of deprivation. On the contrary, it can be just as flavorful, diverse, and satisfying as any other diet.

It's all about redefining your relationship with food. Rather than viewing food as a potential enemy, start seeing it as a trusted ally, a tool you can use to enhance your health and well-being. And that shift in perspective begins with focusing on the positive—on what you can eat, not on what you can't.

There are plenty of foods out there that are gentle on your stomach yet rich in flavors and textures. Fresh fruits and vegetables, lean proteins, whole grains, healthy fats—all these can be part of your reflux-friendly diet. The key is to prepare them in ways that bring out their natural goodness without adding unnecessary acidity or fat.

For instance, you might discover the subtle sweetness of a perfectly roasted sweet potato, the satisfying crunch of a fresh garden salad, or the comforting warmth of a bowl of chicken and rice soup. You might find joy in the vibrant colors of a fruit salad, the tantalizing aroma of baked salmon, or the creamy smoothness of a banana smoothie.

Learning to appreciate these simple, wholesome pleasures can significantly enhance your dining experience, turning each meal into an opportunity for delight and discovery. And when you enjoy your meals, you're more likely to eat mindfully, savoring each bite, which enhances digestion and increases the sense of satiety, preventing overeating.

But the enjoyment of food goes beyond the act of eating. It extends to the entire process of meal planning and preparation. This involves exploring new recipes, experimenting with different ingredients, and honing your cooking skills. It consists in creating a pleasant dining environment, whether setting a beautiful dinner table or enjoying a quiet breakfast by the window.

On this road, remember that the focus is not on perfection but on progress. It's about making small, sustainable changes that make a big difference over time. It's about finding balance, embracing variety, and, most importantly, savoring the joy of eating.

On your path to healthier digestion, it's essential to familiarize yourself with what constitutes a reflux-friendly diet. This diet is not just about restricting or avoiding certain foods. Instead, it's a wholesome approach that focuses on consuming gentle foods on your digestive system while still being delicious and nourishing.

A reflux-friendly diet doesn't require you to eliminate all of your favorite foods. Instead, it encourages you to make thoughtful choices, opting for foods that can reduce the symptoms of acid reflux. It's a commitment to choosing health, comfort, and satisfaction in every meal you consume.

A significant aspect of a reflux-friendly diet is incorporating high-fiber foods. Foods rich in fiber, like whole grains, legumes, and most fruits and vegetables, can absorb excess acid in your stomach, preventing it from flowing back into your esophagus. Moreover, these high-fiber foods aid digestion and promote a feeling of fullness, which helps control overeating, a common trigger for acid reflux.

Lean proteins are also integral to a reflux-friendly diet. Foods like skinless chicken, turkey, fish, and plant-based proteins like lentils and chickpeas provide essential nutrients and digest slowly. This slow digestion prevents your stomach from becoming too full, which can lead to acid reflux.

Healthy fats should also be part of your diet. While it's true that fatty foods can trigger acid reflux, not all fats are created equal. Foods rich in omega-3 fatty acids, like avocados, walnuts, flaxseeds, and cold-water fish like salmon, can help reduce inflammation in your body, including your esophagus.

Now, let's talk portion sizes. Even reflux-friendly foods can cause discomfort if eaten in excess. Therefore, it's essential to practice portion control. A good rule of thumb is to aim for each meal to fit within the size of your two hands cupped together, roughly equivalent to 16-20 ounces.

Hydration is another vital aspect of a reflux-friendly diet. Drinking plenty of water throughout the day not only aids digestion but also dilutes stomach acids, reducing the risk of acid reflux. Just be careful not to consume large quantities of water during meals, as this can increase your stomach volume and potentially trigger reflux.

A reflux-friendly diet is about balance and variety. A well-rounded diet includes a mix of different food groups in the right proportions, ensuring you get a broad range of nutrients while keeping acid reflux at bay.

Everyone is unique, and what works for one person might not work for another. You might need to do a bit of trial and error to figure out what foods you can tolerate and what you can't. Keeping a food diary to track what you eat and how you feel afterward can be a great tool in this process.

Living with GERD or LPR can be challenging. The consistent discomfort, the lifestyle changes, and the worry about triggers can all seem daunting. But it's crucial to remember that you have a significant influence over your well-being. Achieving better digestive health is not only about changing what you eat; it's also about transforming how you think and feel about your condition.

Approaching your digestive health adventure with a positive outlook is the first step to overcoming the obstacles in your way. This mindset does not mean you have to pretend that challenges do not exist; instead, it's about acknowledging the hurdles and focusing on the potential solutions. So, as you dive into the world of reflux-friendly diets, remember to embrace positivity, resilience, and patience.

Just imagine that every step you take brings you closer to discovering the balance that allows you to enjoy your favorite meals, gather with friends and family around the table, and savor every bite without fear of discomfort.

Holding onto a positive outlook can do more than just lift your spirits. Numerous scientific studies suggest a direct correlation between a positive attitude and health outcomes. Positivity can reduce stress, a common trigger for acid reflux. It can improve your resilience to cope with change, making it easier to adapt to new dietary habits. Moreover, positivity can boost your immune system and promote faster recovery.

However, fostering a positive outlook is not always easy, especially when dealing with a chronic condition like GERD or LPR. So, how do you cultivate this positivity? Start by focusing on small wins. Did you try a new reflux-friendly recipe that you enjoyed? That's a win! Did you manage to avoid your acid reflux triggers for a whole day? That's another win!

Maintaining a gratitude journal can also be incredibly helpful. Write down three things you are grateful for daily - they don't have to be big things. Maybe you're thankful for a delicious meal, a supportive friend, or simply a day with less discomfort. This practice can help shift your focus from the negatives and emphasize the positives in your life.

Progress may be slow, and that's okay. Improvements in digestive health do not happen overnight. It's a journey, and every adventure begins with a single step. Some days may be more complex than others, but it's essential not to be too hard on yourself during this process. Celebrate each small victory and learn from the setbacks without letting them deflate your determination.

Staying motivated is essential, and a great way to do that is to set achievable goals. Perhaps it's making it through a week without a significant flare-up, or maybe it's successfully incorporating a new reflux-friendly food into your diet. These goals should be flexible and considerate of your unique journey.

Remember to carry with you a positive outlook. Believe in your strength to face this challenge, and know that each step brings you closer to well-being and joy. Embrace this process with hope and optimism, and keep in mind that you're not alone. Millions of others are walking the same path, and just like them, you too can manage your symptoms, discover delicious foods, and reclaim the joy of eating.

CHAPTER 1: THE ACID REFLUX DIET GUIDELINES

GERD and LPR, while related, present different symptoms and challenges. It's essential to understand what these conditions are and how they can affect you, to move toward better digestive health.

GERD occurs when stomach acid frequently flows back into the tube that connects your mouth and stomach, known as the esophagus. This backwash, or acid reflux, can irritate the lining of your esophagus, causing discomfort. Common symptoms include a burning sensation in your chest, also known as heartburn, and may even leave a sour taste in your mouth. The symptoms usually occur post meals and might worsen when lying flat. You might also experience difficulty swallowing, persistent coughing, or a sensation of a lump in your throat.

On the other hand, LPR, also known as silent reflux, involves the backflow of stomach contents into the larynx, the part of the throat that holds the voice box. Because it doesn't always cause heartburn, LPR can be somewhat tricky to diagnose. It's often the other symptoms, such as hoarseness, a chronic cough, difficulty swallowing, or a sensation of a lump in your throat, that might signal the presence of LPR.

While they might seem intimidating, remember that both GERD and LPR can be managed effectively with appropriate lifestyle modifications, particularly changes in your diet. Understanding these conditions is the first step in recognizing and controlling your triggers, thus reducing your symptoms and enhancing your quality of life.

It's important to note that while some people might have GERD and LPR simultaneously, others might suffer from just one of these conditions. Additionally, everyone experiences these conditions differently. Some people might have severe symptoms but minimal damage to the esophagus or larynx, while others might have significant damage but fewer symptoms. This difference in experience is due to the individual's sensitivity to symptoms and the body's response to reflux.

Although GERD and LPR can significantly impact your lifestyle, it's important to remember that they can be managed, and you're not alone in this journey. Millions of others are grappling with these conditions and are successfully managing their symptoms. With the proper knowledge, a positive outlook, and a committed approach toward a reflux-friendly lifestyle, you can join them in enjoying a symptom-free life.

Knowing how to combat them effectively is just as important as understanding GERD and LPR. A crucial part of this battle involves the food you consume, which brings us to the concept of acid reflux triggers and safe foods. A reflux-friendly diet can significantly impact your comfort and well-being, but it does involve understanding which foods may cause trouble and which can be consumed without worry.

Foods and drinks that commonly trigger acid reflux include alcohol, chocolate, caffeinated beverages, and high-fat or fried foods. These are thought to either relax the lower esophageal sphincter - the ring of muscle that acts as a valve between the esophagus and stomach - or increase the production of stomach acid, both of which can lead to acid reflux.

For instance, let's consider a typical burger and fries meal. The burger, especially if it's high in fat, can cause your stomach to produce more acid. The fries, often deep-fried, contribute to this effect. Add to it a carbonated beverage or a beer, both of which can relax your lower esophageal sphincter, and you've got a perfect recipe for a heartburn episode.

Similarly, spicy foods or those high in citrus content, like oranges or tomatoes, can also contribute to acid reflux. This is because they directly irritate the esophagus lining, causing an uncomfortable burning sensation.

While it might be disheartening to think of avoiding some of your favorite foods, it's important to remember that not all foods will trigger acid reflux. The key is to identify your personal triggers and adjust your diet accordingly.

But it's not all about what you shouldn't eat; let's talk about foods that are generally safe to consume when managing acid reflux. Often referred to as 'safe foods,' they are less likely to cause heartburn and can make a significant difference in managing your symptoms.

Safe foods often include lean proteins like chicken, turkey, or fish, grilled, roasted, or steamed to avoid excess fats. Whole grains, such as oats, brown rice, or whole-grain bread, are also excellent choices. They are high in fiber, absorbing excess acid and aiding digestion.

Non-citrus fruits and most vegetables are also good additions to your diet. Apples, bananas, carrots, and green beans are just a few examples of foods that are less likely to cause reflux. Also, consider healthier cooking methods like grilling, roasting, or steaming instead of frying.

One of the most comforting aspects of embarking on a reflux-friendly diet is discovering that it does not mean you'll be eating bland, uninteresting meals. There's an abundance of delicious and nutrient-dense foods that are less likely to trigger acid reflux.

Let's delve deeper into the food world, examining what items may prompt your acid reflux symptoms and which can help you maintain a more balanced and less disruptive digestive experience. Knowledge is your greatest weapon in managing GERD and LPR, and this comprehensive list aims to empower you to make conscious, informed dietary choices.

Starting with the foods that are best avoided or limited, keep in mind that these may trigger acid reflux for many people, but everyone is unique. Your body might react differently, but here's a solid starting point.

High-fat foods are problematic for your stomach to digest, leading to a potential overload of stomach acid. Common culprits include fatty cuts of meat, full-fat dairy, and fried or greasy foods. Yes, this may, unfortunately, include your favorite fast-food items.

Citrus fruits: oranges, lemons, grapefruits, and their juices can increase acid production and irritate your esophagus. An apple or banana might be a safer bet when you're looking for a quick snack.

Spicy foods: while they might set your taste buds on fire in the best way, they can also trigger acid reflux. Hot peppers and hot sauces are usual suspects, but any food that has a kick could be a potential trigger.

Caffeine: found in more than just your morning cup of Joe, caffeine can be found in certain teas, chocolate, some pain relievers, and other beverages like sodas and energy drinks.

Alcohol: like caffeine, alcohol can relax the lower esophageal sphincter and stimulate acid production, significantly triggering many people.

Let us now turn to foods that can be your allies in improving digestive health.

Lean proteins: grilled chicken, turkey, fish, or lean cuts of meat are excellent choices. These provide you with the necessary proteins without the excess fats that could provoke your acid reflux.

Whole grains: foods like brown rice, oatmeal, whole-grain bread, and whole-grain pasta are great options. They provide you with the necessary fiber, which aids in digestion and can absorb excess stomach acid.

Non-acidic fruits and vegetables: think apples, bananas, carrots, peas, leafy greens, and green beans. These foods are less likely to trigger acid reflux and are filled with essential nutrients your body needs.

Healthy fats: avocados, walnuts, flaxseeds, and olive oil are examples of more beneficial fats that your body needs for optimal function. These can be used in moderation without the same potential for triggering acid reflux as less healthy fats.

Herbal teas: chamomile, licorice root, and slippery elm have been used for centuries to soothe upset stomachs and could potentially help ease GERD symptoms.

In your journey to better manage GERD and LPR, you'll find these lists of potential trigger foods and safer alternatives a helpful starting point. But remember, you're an individual, and your body might not react the same way as others. Learning to listen to your body's signals is a vital aspect of this process, which brings us to the next point: the role of portion control.

As you explore the world of reflux-friendly foods, another key aspect that you should pay attention to is portion control. You might wonder why, if you're consuming the right foods, does the amount matter? It matters because an overloaded stomach can easily lead to acid reflux, no matter how healthy the food is. Even the most reflux-friendly diet can backfire without proper portion management.

The stomach is roughly the size of your clenched fist and is designed to hold about one quart of food at any given time. When you consume more than this, your stomach stretches, putting pressure on the lower esophageal sphincter (LES). The LES is a ring of muscle that acts like a valve, keeping the contents of your stomach, including the acid, from flowing back up into the esophagus. When the LES is under pressure, it can weaken and open, allowing acid to reflux into your esophagus and cause the uncomfortable symptoms you know all too well.

So, how can you practice portion control? Here are some valuable tips.

Smaller Meals, More Often: instead of three large meals, try having five to six smaller meals spread throughout the day. This will prevent your stomach from becoming too full and reduce the risk of reflux.

Use Smaller Plates and Bowls: this simple visual trick can help you consume less. When you use a smaller plate, a modest portion looks more substantial, which can help you feel satisfied with less.

Mindful Eating: take time to chew your food thoroughly and enjoy each bite. Not only will this help you savor your food more, but it will also give your body time to register fullness, preventing overeating.

Measure Your Servings: it can be easy to overestimate portion sizes, especially when you're hungry. Use measuring cups or a digital food scale to ensure you're getting just the right amount. Remember, a serving of meat, fish, or poultry should be about the size of a deck of cards or 3-4 oz, a serving of grains should be about 1/2 cup, and a serving of fruit is typically one medium piece or 1/2 cup chopped.

Stay Hydrated: sometimes, we mistake thirst for hunger. Ensure you're drinking enough water throughout the day (but not during meals, as this can dilute stomach acids and lead to reflux). Aiming for at least eight 8-ounce glasses of water daily is a good goal.

Listen to Your Body: eat when you're hungry, but stop when you're satisfied, not full. If you feel overstuffed, you've likely overeaten.

The beauty of these tips is that they are easy to implement and can be tailored to your lifestyle. Over time, they will become second nature, and your body will thank you. Managing GERD and LPR is a marathon, not a sprint. The next part of this pathway is to delve into the impact of your overall eating habits and lifestyle on your digestive health.

Embarking on a journey towards improved digestion involves not just dietary changes, but also modifications in your eating habits and overall lifestyle. These shifts in your daily routine can significantly contribute to managing GERD and LPR symptoms. It's not just about what you eat, but also how and when you eat, as well as other habits that can impact digestion.

Start by focusing on your eating routine. Are you eating on the go or at your desk while working? Eating mindfully can make a huge difference in your digestion. This means sitting down to eat, avoiding distractions like TV or phones, and focusing on your meal. Take the time to chew your food well. Digestion starts in the mouth, and the more you break down the food there, the less work your stomach has to do.

Next, consider your meal timing. Try to keep a regular eating schedule and avoid eating too close to bedtime. Ideally, you should finish eating at least 3 hours before you go to bed to give your body sufficient time to digest the food. Lying down with a full stomach can lead to reflux, as gravity no longer helps to keep the food and stomach acid down.

Beyond your eating habits, other lifestyle changes can significantly impact digestion. For example, maintaining a healthy weight is crucial. Extra pounds, especially around your abdomen, can pressure your stomach and cause acid back into your esophagus. Regular exercise, combined with a balanced diet, can help you reach and maintain a healthy weight.

Smoking and alcohol consumption can also worsen GERD and LPR symptoms. Smoking damages the LES, making it less effective at keeping stomach acid where it belongs. Alcohol, meanwhile, can relax the LES and stimulate the production of stomach acid. Reducing or quitting these habits can significantly improve your symptoms if you smoke or drink regularly.

Stress management is another important aspect of digestion. High stress or anxiety levels can lead to increased acid production in the stomach, leading to reflux. Finding healthy ways to manage stress is crucial, such as regular physical activity, relaxation techniques like meditation or deep-breathing exercises, or simply engaging in hobbies you enjoy.

Lastly, consider the way you sleep. If you suffer from night-time reflux, elevating the head of your bed or using a wedge pillow can be helpful. By raising your upper body, you can utilize gravity to help keep stomach acid from flowing back into the esophagus while you sleep.

Remember, it's the little changes that, when added together, can significantly impact your overall digestive health. The goal is to cultivate habits that sustainably promote a reflux-friendly lifestyle. As you continue on this path, you'll better understand how different lifestyle elements affect your digestive health and become better equipped to manage your symptoms effectively.

CHAPTER 2: CREATING A GERD AND LPR-FRIENDLY KITCHEN

The path to conquering GERD and LPR doesn't stop at the grocery store. The following essential stop is your kitchen. Just as your body is your temple, your kitchen is the heart of your home, where you'll make the magic happen. In your mission to manage acid reflux, efficiently organizing your kitchen can be a significant boon.

Imagine this: you're in a rush to prepare a meal. Your stomach's grumbling, and your reflux symptoms are on high alert. The stress can amplify your symptoms if you're scrambling to find ingredients or tools. An organized kitchen can be your silent ally in these moments. It brings order to your cooking process, reduces meal preparation time, and creates an environment that makes it easier to stick to your reflux-friendly diet.

Start by arranging your food storage areas — the fridge, freezer, and pantry. You want to ensure that the foods you need for your reflux-friendly diet are easily accessible. Place your safe foods at eye level so they're the first things you see. This can help resist the temptation to reach for reflux triggers.

Group similar items together, like all the whole grains in one spot and all the fresh produce in another. The goal is to know exactly where every ingredient is. This doesn't just save time during meal preparation; it also helps you keep track of what you have, reducing waste and unnecessary purchases.

Next, take a look at your cookware and utensils. Are they easy to reach? Often, you might need a specific tool quickly in the heat of cooking. Having your most-used items within arm's reach can make cooking smoother and more enjoyable. Consider keeping a container on your countertop with essential tools like wooden spoons, spatulas, and tongs.

It's not just about organization, however. Having the right tools can make a big difference too. Investing in a good quality, non-stick pan can help you cook with less oil, while a slow cooker can be a lifesaver for preparing make-ahead meals that are ready when you are, saving you from potential bouts of hunger-induced acid reflux.

Your spice rack deserves some attention too. Spices can significantly enhance the flavor of your food without triggering reflux. However, they should be used wisely as some can irritate your condition. Store your safe spices front and center, making them easy to reach for when cooking.

It's essential to keep your kitchen clean. A clean kitchen is a pleasant environment that encourages you to cook. Not only that, but it also reduces the risk of food contamination. Cleaning as you go can prevent tasks from piling up and becoming overwhelming, which can trigger stress and potentially worsen your symptoms.

An organized kitchen is about creating an environment that supports your dietary changes. When your kitchen works with you, not against you, sticking to a reflux-friendly diet becomes more manageable. As you go through this journey, take comfort in knowing that every step you take, even seemingly small ones like organizing your kitchen, brings you closer to better managing your GERD and LPR symptoms.

When it comes to building a refuge from acid reflux in your own home, a well-stocked pantry can be your strongest fortress. Filling your shelves with reflux-friendly foods not only makes meal preparation easier but also helps ensure you have safe food options readily at hand when hunger strikes.

Start with the basics – whole grains. Whole grains like brown rice, quinoa, and oats are not only rich in fiber, which can aid digestion, but also have a relatively low acidity level. Opt for whole-grain versions of pasta and bread for more variety. Store them in airtight containers to maintain freshness, and if space allows, keep an extra package on hand so you're never caught off-guard.

Your pantry should also include a variety of legumes, such as lentils, chickpeas, and black beans. They're high in protein and fiber and can be easily added to salads, soups, and stews. Canned varieties can be a lifesaver when you need a quick meal, but be sure to rinse them thoroughly to remove any excess sodium.

Next, think about your cooking fats. Olive oil is an excellent choice as it's not only reflux-friendly but also loaded with heart-healthy monounsaturated fats. While it's perfect for sautéing and roasting, it can also be used in dressings and marinades. Despite being a saturated fat, coconut oil is another good option for cooking at high temperatures.

Don't forget about nuts and seeds. For instance, almonds, walnuts, and chia seeds are high in fiber and healthy fats. They make excellent snacks, salad toppings, or additions to your morning oatmeal. However, nuts can be high in fat, so be mindful of portion sizes – a handful (about 1 oz) is usually enough for a snack.

Herbs and spices are vital for adding flavor without the heat that can trigger reflux. Keep a variety of these on hand, such as oregano, thyme, and ginger. Turmeric, with its anti-inflammatory properties, can also be a beneficial addition.

For a hint of sweetness, consider having honey in your pantry. It's a natural sweetener that can soothe the throat and possibly neutralize acid in your esophagus. Other options include maple syrup and agave nectar. Be mindful, however, that all sweeteners should be used sparingly.

Canned fish, like tuna and salmon, are excellent sources of lean protein and omega-3 fatty acids. They can be a quick and easy addition to salads or pasta, making for a swift, reflux-friendly meal.

Finally, stock up on reflux-friendly beverages. Herbal teas like chamomile and ginger can help soothe your stomach and reduce acid reflux symptoms. Alternatively, opt for non-citrus fruit juices, or better yet, make water your go-to beverage.

Everyone's triggers are unique, so use this list as a starting point and adjust according to your body's responses. Over time, you'll build a pantry tailored to your needs, turning your kitchen into a true refuge from acid reflux. The power to manage your GERD and LPR is at your fingertips, right inside your pantry door.

To make your kitchen a haven for managing GERD and LPR, you shouldn't overlook the importance of the tools you use to prepare your meals. As with your pantry, carefully selecting your kitchen utensils can greatly enhance reflux-friendly cooking. With the right tools at your disposal, you can make the process of preparing and enjoying reflux-friendly meals easier, more efficient, and more enjoyable.

Start by taking a look at your cookware. Certain materials can impact the healthfulness of your meals. For instance, consider using stainless steel pots and pans. These are durable, easy to clean, and don't leach harmful chemicals into your food as some non-stick pans can. Cast iron is another great option, particularly for high-heat cooking. While it requires a bit more care to maintain, it provides an excellent, naturally non-stick surface once correctly seasoned.

When it comes to bakeware, opt for glass or ceramic dishes. They're non-reactive, meaning they won't leach any substances into your food when exposed to acidic or alkaline ingredients, ensuring your meals stay reflux-friendly.

Now, let's talk about knives. A high-quality, sharp chef's knife can make all the difference in your food preparation. It will make chopping easier, more efficient, and safer. You'll also need a good paring knife for smaller tasks and possibly a serrated knife for slicing bread and tomatoes.

Consider investing in a food processor or blender, which can help in preparing reflux-friendly sauces, soups, and smoothies without any irritating chunks. They can also be used for chopping and slicing, reducing the time and effort you need to put into meal preparation.

Having a good set of wooden or silicone utensils is also beneficial. Unlike metal utensils, they won't scratch your cookware. They're ideal for stirring, flipping, and serving. Silicone utensils, in particular, are heat-resistant and won't melt if you leave them in the pot or pan.

A slow cooker can be a godsend, especially for those busy days when you don't have time to cook a meal from scratch. You can throw in your ingredients in the morning, set it, and come home to a hot, ready-to-eat meal. Plus, slow cooking can make your meals more flavorful without the need for reflux-triggering spices.

In terms of storage, glass containers are your best bet. They are free from harmful chemicals often found in plastic containers, and they won't retain odors or stains. Being microwave safe, they make reheating leftovers easy and convenient.

Lastly, don't underestimate the importance of a good quality, accurate kitchen scale. It's crucial for portion control, ensuring you don't overeat reflux-triggering foods. Look for one that's easy to clean and has a clear, easy-to-read display.

Remember, your kitchen is your sanctuary. The utensils you use should support and enhance your reflux-friendly cooking efforts. With the right tools, you can make your meals enjoyable, healthy, and, most importantly, discomfort-free.

Navigating the path to reflux-friendly cooking can be daunting, but it can become second nature with the proper techniques and tips. The key is to focus on preparing meals to minimize acid reflux triggers. So, where do you begin?

Firstly, let's address the issue of cooking methods. Certain methods can elevate the fat content of your food, potentially exacerbating your symptoms. Instead, opt for techniques like grilling, steaming, roasting, and baking, which require little to no added fat. Stir-frying can be an option, too, provided you use minimal oil.

Spices can be a double-edged sword when it comes to seasoning your meals. While they add flavor, they can also trigger acid reflux. Therefore, try to find a balance by using mild herbs and spices. Subtle flavors from thyme, rosemary, and sage, or sweetness from cinnamon and nutmeg, can offer a flavorful punch without irritating your stomach. Experiment with different herbs and spices to find what works best for you.

Now, about your ingredients. Always remember to rinse canned vegetables, beans, and legumes to wash away any additional sodium that might be present. Sodium can cause bloating and discomfort, which can worsen reflux symptoms. Fresh produce is always the best choice, but when you do use canned goods, this step can make a significant difference.

Speaking of produce, did you know roasting or grilling your fruits and vegetables can help reduce their acidity? Techniques like these can make tomatoes, citrus fruits, and other typically off-limits foods more tolerable for some.

When it comes to meat, opt for lean cuts and make sure to trim any visible fat before cooking. Fat can slow down digestion, leading to an overproduction of stomach acid. Similarly, choose low-fat dairy products whenever possible.

Portion control is another critical factor. Large meals can put pressure on your lower esophageal sphincter (the muscle that keeps stomach acid from moving into your esophagus), leading to reflux. Instead, aim for smaller, more frequent meals throughout the day.

Let's not forget about beverages. Try to avoid drinks that are high in caffeine or carbonation, as these can trigger acid reflux. Instead, hydrate with water or herbal teas. Chamomile and ginger teas, in particular, have soothing properties that may help ease reflux symptoms.

When baking, look for ways to reduce the fat content. Applesauce or mashed bananas can be excellent substitutes for oil or butter in many recipes. And for added flavor, consider adding a bit of vanilla extract.

Lastly, don't rush the cooking process. High heat can cause food to cook unevenly, potentially creating tough, harder-to-digest textures. Cooking your food slowly and thoroughly can help retain its natural flavors and make it easier on your stomach.

Taking these cooking tips and techniques to heart will guide you toward creating meals that are delicious, satisfying, and, more importantly, conducive to managing your GERD and LPR symptoms. You're not just cooking meals, you're preparing a foundation for better digestive health, and every positive step you take in the kitchen is a step towards a life free of discomfort and full of joy.

Cleanliness in the kitchen is about more than just keeping your space tidy; it is an integral part of ensuring a reflux-friendly environment by preventing cross-contamination. This is especially important if you're sharing your kitchen with others who may be using ingredients that are not reflux-friendly. The last thing you want is traces of potential trigger foods winding up in your carefully crafted meals. So, let's delve into some essential tips to help you maintain a clean and safe kitchen environment.

Your first line of defense against cross-contamination is establishing separate zones for different types of foods. If possible, allocate specific areas of your refrigerator and pantry for your reflux-friendly ingredients. This way, you can ensure that these items don't come into contact with potential triggers.

You can also consider color-coding your utensils, cutting boards, and dishes. For example, you might use blue items to prepare fruits and vegetables and red items to handle trigger foods. This practice can help you quickly identify which tools are safe to use and which ones need to be washed before use.

Cleaning as you go can significantly reduce the risk of cross-contamination. Every time you finish using a cutting board or knife, take a moment to clean it thoroughly with warm, soapy water, rinse it, and let it air dry or dry it with a clean towel. Don't forget to clean your countertops and stovetops regularly, especially before and after food preparation.

Hand hygiene is another crucial factor. Make sure to wash your hands with warm soapy water for at least 20 seconds before and after handling food, especially after touching potentially triggering foods. And don't overlook the more minor details — your nails can harbor germs too. Keep them short and clean to avoid transferring any bacteria to your food.

Moreover, paying attention to your dishcloths and sponges is vital. These are often overlooked, but they can be a breeding ground for bacteria. Make sure to replace your sponges regularly and wash your dishcloths frequently. Consider using paper towels for cleaning surfaces where you've prepared trigger foods.

Remember to keep your appliances clean as well. From your blender to your toaster, ensure that these are free from food particles that could contaminate your next meal. Pay particular attention to your microwave — food splatters can build up over time and potentially contaminate your reflux-friendly meals.

You should also be mindful of storage. After cooking, don't leave your food out for more than two hours. Instead, store it in airtight containers in the refrigerator or freezer. Also, check your refrigerator temperature regularly. It should be at or below 40 degrees Fahrenheit to slow bacterial growth.

These steps might seem like a lot to take on, but don't feel overwhelmed. Just like learning to cook with reflux-friendly methods, maintaining a clean kitchen to prevent cross-contamination is a process. Little by little, you'll establish habits that ensure your kitchen is not just a place where food is prepared but a place where your well-being is safeguarded. By adhering to these cleanliness tips, you're making another stride towards a more comfortable and enjoyable eating experience. After all, food should be your ally, not your enemy. Through these practices, you're turning your kitchen into a fortress against GERD and LPR, paving the way to better health.

CHAPTER 3: FLAVORFUL BREAKFAST RECIPES

The saying, "Breakfast is the most important meal of the day," holds much truth, especially when you're navigating the terrain of GERD and LPR. Your first meal sets the stage for your eating patterns throughout the day. Choosing reflux-friendly options for breakfast can help you manage your symptoms and start your day on the right note.

Now, you might wonder, "Why is breakfast so essential for managing GERD and LPR?" Here's the answer: Overnight, while you sleep, your stomach continues to produce acid. If you skip breakfast, this acid doesn't have any food to work on, which can lead to heartburn and discomfort. A wholesome breakfast helps neutralize this stomach acid and provides a buffer, reducing the chances of reflux.

Consider this — it's not just about having breakfast but also about what you eat for breakfast. Aim to have a meal that's high in fiber and includes a lean protein source. Foods rich in fiber, like oatmeal or whole grain bread, can absorb excess stomach acid and help in its slow release, preventing a sudden surge that can trigger GERD or LPR symptoms. Pairing this with a lean protein, like eggs or plant-based options like tofu or beans, provides a steady energy source that can help prevent the hunger pangs, which could lead to overeating later in the day — another potential trigger for acid reflux.

When choosing your breakfast components, be aware of the foods that typically trigger GERD or LPR. For example, consider leaner options like turkey bacon or lean ham instead of high-fat meats like sausage or bacon. If dairy products start your symptoms, consider alternatives like almond milk or soy milk for your cereal or coffee. Be creative and experiment with different options until you find what works best for you.

Portion size matters, even at breakfast. Overeating can put pressure on the lower esophageal sphincter (LES), the muscle that prevents stomach contents from moving back into the esophagus, causing it to open and lead to acid reflux. Aim for moderate portions to start your day without overwhelming your stomach or the LES.

Timing your breakfast is another aspect to consider. Try to eat your breakfast for at least three hours before lying down or exercising to allow your body enough time to digest the meal and reduce the chance of reflux.

Hydration is another essential element. Starting your day with a glass of water aids in digestion, hydrating your body after a night's sleep. However, avoid drinking large amounts of liquid with your meal as it can distend the stomach and trigger reflux.

The way to a healthier breakfast can seem daunting. But remember, change is a process. It doesn't happen overnight. Take your time to understand your body and what works best for you. This is not about a stringent diet or deprivation; instead, it's about making healthier choices that help manage your GERD and LPR symptoms.

In time, you'll realize that these changes help manage your reflux symptoms and contribute to your overall well-being. A nourishing, reflux-friendly breakfast can give you the energy and comfort you need to start your day, enabling you to enjoy the rest of your day without worrying about triggering your GERD or LPR. After all, the goal is to live a whole and joyful life where food is an ally in your wellness journey, not a foe. Embrace breakfast, embrace wellness!

Breakfast smoothie recipes

Smoothies can be an incredible addition to your breakfast routine, especially when managing GERD and LPR. They are easily digestible, versatile, and a great way to pack in various reflux-friendly foods. Here, let's dive into some delicious and nutrient-dense breakfast smoothie recipes to help you start your day with a delightful and, most importantly, reflux-free morning.

1. Almond Banana Smoothie

Ingredients:

1 banana
1 cup almond milk (8 oz)
2 tablespoons almond butter
1 tablespoon honey
1/2 teaspoon vanilla extract

Peel the banana, and add it to your blender along with the almond milk, almond butter, honey, and vanilla extract. Blend until smooth, and enjoy a creamy, comforting breakfast that's gentle on your stomach.

2. Berry Oatmeal Smoothie

Ingredients:

1/2 cup rolled oats (4 oz)
1 cup mixed berries (strawberries, blueberries, raspberries - 8 oz)
1 cup Greek yogurt (8 oz)
1 tablespoon honey

Start by blending the oats until they form a fine powder. Add in the berries, Greek yogurt, and honey. Blend until smooth and enjoy the tartness of berries balanced with the creaminess of yogurt and oats.

3. Green Goddess Smoothie

Ingredients:

1 cup spinach (8 oz)
1/2 avocado
1 banana
1 cup almond milk (8 oz)
1 tablespoon honey

Combine the spinach, avocado, banana, almond milk, and honey in a blender. Blend until smooth and creamy. This smoothie is a powerhouse of essential nutrients and a beautiful start to the day.

4. Ginger Pear Smoothie

Ingredients:

1 pear
1 small piece of fresh ginger
1 cup Greek yogurt (8 oz)
1 tablespoon honey

Core the pear and chop it into pieces. Add the pear, ginger, Greek yogurt, and honey to the blender and blend until smooth. This refreshing smoothie is bound to invigorate your senses.

5. Chia Seed Tropical Smoothie

Ingredients:

1 cup coconut milk (8 oz)
1 banana
1/2 cup pineapple chunks (4 oz)
1 tablespoon chia seeds
Combine the coconut milk, banana, pineapple chunks, and chia seeds in a blender. Blend until you reach a smooth consistency. This tropical delight will transport your taste buds to a beachy paradise.

6. Vanilla Cinnamon Smoothie

Ingredients:

1 banana
1 cup almond milk (8 oz)
1 tablespoon honey
1 teaspoon cinnamon
1/2 teaspoon vanilla extract

Peel the banana, and put it in your blender along with almond milk, honey, cinnamon, and vanilla extract. Blend until smooth and savor the subtle spice from cinnamon combined with the natural sweetness of banana and honey.

7. Blueberry Apple Smoothie

Ingredients:

1 cup blueberries (8 oz)
1 apple
1 cup Greek yogurt (8 oz)
1 tablespoon honey

Core the apple and cut it into pieces. Add the apple pieces, blueberries, Greek yogurt, and honey to your blender. Blend until smooth and enjoy this nutrient-packed smoothie with the tartness of blueberries balanced with the sweetness of apples.

8. Mango Avocado Smoothie

Ingredients:

1 ripe mango
1/2 avocado
1 cup coconut milk (8 oz)
1 tablespoon honey

Peel and pit the mango and avocado. Add them to your blender with the coconut milk and honey. Blend until smooth and creamy. This tropical smoothie is a real treat to your taste buds while also being easy on your digestion.

9. Oatmeal Peach Smoothie

Ingredients:

1 peach
1/2 cup rolled oats (4 oz)
1 cup almond milk (8 oz)
1 tablespoon honey

Blend the oats until they form a fine powder. Add in the peach (pitted and cut into pieces), almond milk, and honey. Blend until smooth. This smoothie is a perfect balance of natural sweetness and hearty oats.

10. Spinach Pineapple Smoothie

Ingredients:

1 cup spinach (8 oz)
1/2 cup pineapple chunks (4 oz)
1 banana
1 cup almond milk (8 oz)

Add the spinach, pineapple chunks, banana, and almond milk to your blender. Blend until you reach a smooth and creamy consistency. This green smoothie is not just delicious but also packed with essential nutrients.

As you start blending, remember that smoothies are easily customizable. If you find a particular ingredient doesn't sit well with your stomach, feel free to replace it or remove it from the recipe. Equally, you can get creative by adding your favorite safe fruits or even sneaking in some vegetables for an extra nutrient punch.

Preparation tip: prepare your fruits and veggies the night before and store them in the refrigerator. This way, you can just toss them into the blender in the morning, saving you precious time during your morning routine.

Smoothies offer a quick and delicious breakfast option, allowing you to experiment with various textures and flavors, keeping your breakfast exciting and enjoyable. Each sip delivers essential nutrients to your body and helps ease your GERD and LPR symptoms, supporting your journey to improved digestive health. Start your day right with these refreshing smoothies and feel the difference in your overall well-being. Enjoy blending!

Oatmeal recipes

No breakfast food feels quite as comforting and satisfying as oatmeal. Packed with soluble fiber, it's not only good for your heart, but it's also gentle on your stomach, making it an ideal breakfast for those dealing with GERD and LPR. The recipes shared here are crafted to be reflux-friendly, considering the balance of flavors and the need to avoid potential trigger foods.

1. Classic Oatmeal with a Twist

Ingredients:

1 cup rolled oats (8 oz)
2 cups almond milk (16 oz)
A pinch of salt
1 tablespoon honey
1/4 teaspoon cinnamon
A handful of blueberries

Cook oats with almond milk and a pinch of salt on medium heat. Once the oats are tender and have absorbed the milk, remove them from heat. Stir in honey and cinnamon. Top with a handful of fresh blueberries. The result is a comforting bowl of oatmeal with the perfect balance of sweetness and the refreshing taste of blueberries.

2. Overnight Oats with Chia Seeds

Ingredients:

1/2 cup rolled oats (4 oz)
1 cup almond milk (8 oz)
1 tablespoon chia seeds
1 tablespoon maple syrup
Sliced bananas for topping

Combine oats, almond milk, chia seeds, and maple syrup in a jar. Stir well, cover the pot, and refrigerate overnight. In the morning, stir it well and top it with banana slices. These overnight oats with chia seeds offer a texture-rich take on traditional oatmeal with the convenience of a ready-to-eat breakfast.

3. Savory Oatmeal with Avocado

Ingredients:

1 cup rolled oats (8 oz)
2 cups water
A pinch of salt
1/2 ripe avocado, sliced
A sprinkle of black pepper

Cook oats with water and a pinch of salt. Once cooked, place the oatmeal in a bowl, top with avocado slices, and sprinkle with black pepper. Savory oatmeal is a nourishing way to start the day, and adding avocado introduces a source of healthy fats.

4. Pumpkin Spice Oatmeal

Ingredients:

1 cup rolled oats (8 oz)
2 cups almond milk (16 oz)
A pinch of salt
1/4 cup pureed pumpkin (2 oz)

1/4 teaspoon pumpkin spice
1 tablespoon maple syrup

Cook oats with almond milk and a pinch of salt. Once the oats are cooked, stir in the pumpkin puree, pumpkin spice, and maple syrup. This seasonal oatmeal recipe is perfect for those cozy fall mornings.

5. Apple Cinnamon Oatmeal

Ingredients:

1 cup rolled oats (8 oz)
2 cups almond milk (16 oz)
A pinch of salt
1 apple, diced
1/4 teaspoon cinnamon
1 tablespoon honey

Cook oats with almond milk and a pinch of salt. Once the oats are cooked, stir in diced apple, cinnamon, and honey. Enjoy this warming, apple-cinnamon-flavored oatmeal.

6. Pear and Ginger Oatmeal

Ingredients:

1 cup rolled oats (8 oz)
2 cups almond milk (16 oz)
A pinch of salt
1 ripe pear, diced
1/4 teaspoon ground ginger
1 tablespoon honey

Cook the oats with almond milk and a pinch of salt. Once cooked, stir in the diced pear, ground ginger, and honey. This bowl of oatmeal balances the gentle heat of ginger with the sweetness of ripe pear.

7. Oatmeal with Almond Butter and Banana
Ingredients:

1 cup rolled oats (8 oz)
2 cups water
A pinch of salt
1 tablespoon almond butter
1 banana, sliced

Cook the oats with water and a pinch of salt. Once cooked, stir in the almond butter until it's well incorporated. Top the oatmeal with banana slices. This is a creamy and filling breakfast option.

8. Tropical Oatmeal

Ingredients:

1 cup rolled oats (8 oz)
2 cups coconut milk (16 oz)
A pinch of salt
1/4 cup diced pineapple
1/4 cup shredded coconut

Cook the oats with coconut milk and a pinch of salt. Once cooked, stir in the diced pineapple and shredded coconut. This oatmeal will transport you to the tropics with its vibrant flavors.

9. Oatmeal with Raisins and Cinnamon
Ingredients:

1 cup rolled oats (8 oz)
2 cups almond milk (16 oz)
A pinch of salt
1/4 cup raisins
1/4 teaspoon cinnamon
1 tablespoon maple syrup

Cook the oats with almond milk and a pinch of salt. Once cooked, stir in the raisins, cinnamon, and maple syrup. This is a classic oatmeal combination, reminiscent of a warm cinnamon roll.

10. Cherry Almond Oatmeal

Ingredients:

1 cup rolled oats (8 oz)
2 cups almond milk (16 oz)
A pinch of salt
1/4 cup dried cherries
1/4 cup sliced almonds
1 tablespoon honey

Cook the oats with almond milk and a pinch of salt. Once cooked, stir in the dried cherries, sliced almonds, and honey. This oatmeal combines tart cherries and crunchy almonds for a satisfying texture contrast.

These oatmeal recipes can be adjusted to meet your personal taste preferences and dietary needs. By starting your day with a wholesome bowl of oatmeal, you're not only fueling your body with nutrient-rich foods, but also taking a step towards managing your GERD and LPR symptoms. Enjoy these comforting oatmeal bowls, and start your day feeling nourished and well-cared-for.

Egg-based dishes

Eggs are a powerhouse of nutrition, packed with essential proteins, vitamins, and minerals. While they can be enjoyed in many ways, it's vital to remember that for managing GERD and LPR, some cooking methods are better than others. When preparing egg-based dishes, aim for processes that require minimal oil or butter, such as poaching or hard-boiling, and avoid heavy spices.

1. Poached Eggs with Avocado

The humble poached egg is a delicious, protein-packed start to your day. Paired with avocado, which provides healthy fats and fiber, it makes for a well-rounded breakfast.

Ingredients:

2 large eggs
1 ripe avocado
2 slices of whole grain bread
Salt and pepper to taste

Start by poaching the eggs in gently simmering water. While the eggs are poaching, toast your bread and slice your avocado. Top each piece of toast with half of the avocado and a poached egg. Season with a light sprinkle of salt and pepper to taste.

2. Hard-Boiled Eggs with Quinoa Salad

A hard-boiled egg, with its firm whites and creamy yolk, can be a simple yet satisfying meal. Pairing it with a quinoa salad adds a variety of textures and flavors while boosting the meal's fiber content.

Ingredients:

2 large eggs
1 cup cooked quinoa (6 oz)
A handful of fresh spinach
A handful of cherry tomatoes, halved
Salt and pepper to taste

Begin by hard-boiling the eggs. While the eggs boil, prepare your quinoa salad by combining the cooked quinoa, fresh spinach, and cherry tomatoes. Once the eggs are done, peel them and slice them in half, arranging them on top of your quinoa salad. Add salt and pepper to taste.

3. Scrambled Eggs with Fresh Herbs

Scrambled eggs are a breakfast classic. They can be a reflux-friendly option when prepared without excess butter or cream. Fresh herbs add a burst of flavor without contributing to acid reflux symptoms.

Ingredients:

2 large eggs
A splash of almond milk
A handful of fresh herbs, such as parsley or chives, chopped
Salt and pepper to taste

Crack your eggs into a bowl, add a splash of almond milk, and whisk until well combined. Heat a non-stick pan over medium heat and pour in the eggs. Stir gently until the eggs are cooked to your desired consistency. Just before they're done, stir in the fresh herbs and season with a touch of salt and pepper.

4. Veggie Omelet

An omelet is a versatile dish that can be filled with various ingredients. Choose non-acidic vegetables like bell peppers, zucchini, and spinach for a reflux-friendly version.

Ingredients:

2 large eggs
A splash of almond milk
1/4 bell pepper, diced
1/4 zucchini, diced
A handful of fresh spinach
Salt and pepper to taste

Begin by sautéing the bell pepper and zucchini in a non-stick pan until softened. In a separate bowl, whisk the eggs with a splash of almond milk. Pour the eggs over the vegetables, spreading them out evenly. Once the bottom of the omelet is set, scatter the spinach on top and fold the omelet over. Continue cooking until the eggs are fully set, then season with a touch of salt and pepper.

5. Avocado and Egg White Scramble

Light, fluffy, and packed with protein, this scramble is a great way to start the day.

Ingredients:

4 egg whites
1 ripe avocado
Salt and pepper to taste

Begin by whisking the egg whites until frothy. Cook them in a non-stick pan over medium heat, stirring occasionally. When the eggs are almost cooked, stir in the diced avocado. Season with a pinch of salt and pepper.

6. Baked Eggs with Asparagus

This dish is a simple yet elegant breakfast that's easy to prepare.

Ingredients:

2 large eggs
6 spears of asparagus, trimmed
Salt and pepper to taste

Preheat your oven to 350°F. Arrange the asparagus in a baking dish and crack the eggs on top. Bake until the egg whites are set but the yolks are still runny, about 15 minutes. Season with a bit of salt and pepper.

7. Egg, Tomato, and Basil Open-Face Sandwich

A light and fresh breakfast option, this sandwich is bursting with flavor.

Ingredients:

1 large egg
1 slice of whole grain bread
1 small tomato, sliced

A few fresh basil leaves
Salt and pepper to taste

Start by cooking the egg to your preference (a fried or poached egg works well here). Toast the bread, then top it with the sliced tomato, cooked egg, and fresh basil leaves. Season with a touch of salt and pepper.

8. Sweet Potato and Egg Breakfast Hash

This nutrient-dense breakfast is satisfying and delicious, filled with complex carbs and protein.

Ingredients:

2 large eggs
1 small sweet potato, diced (about 8 oz)
Salt and pepper to taste

In a non-stick pan, cook the sweet potato until it's softened and slightly caramelized. In another pan, cook the eggs to your preference (scrambled or fried would work well). Combine the eggs and sweet potato in a bowl and season with a bit of salt and pepper.

9. Mediterranean Egg Muffins

These savory muffins are a convenient and portable breakfast option, perfect for busy mornings.

Ingredients:

6 large eggs
1 cup diced bell peppers (about 5 oz)
1/2 cup diced zucchini (about 4 oz)
A handful of fresh spinach, chopped
Salt and pepper to taste

Preheat your oven to 350°F and grease a muffin tin. In a bowl, whisk the eggs and add the diced vegetables and spinach. Season with salt and pepper. Pour the mixture into the muffin tin and bake for 20-25 minutes, or until the eggs are set.

10. Quinoa and Veggie Scramble

This protein-packed scramble pairs quinoa with eggs for a filling and nutritious start to the day.

Ingredients:

4 large egg whites
1/2 cup cooked quinoa (about 4 oz)
A mix of your favorite veggies (bell peppers, zucchini, and spinach work well)
Salt and pepper to taste

Start by whisking the egg whites until frothy. Cook them in a non-stick pan over medium heat, stirring occasionally. When the eggs are almost done, stir in the cooked quinoa and diced veggies. Cook until everything is heated through and the veggies are slightly softened. Season with a pinch of salt and pepper.

With this dish, you're getting a balance of lean protein, complex carbs, and veggies for a breakfast that will satisfy you throughout the morning. As with all the recipes, remember to listen to your body and adjust the ingredients as needed to suit your specific dietary needs.

These recipes should offer a diverse range of options to keep your breakfasts enjoyable and reflux-friendly. Always moderate the quantities to your dietary needs and listen to your body's response to different foods.

Reflux-friendly breakfast beverages

As you stride into the kitchen, the first light of dawn peeking in through the window, you might find yourself reaching for your usual morning cup of joe or black tea. But wait, those might not be the most suitable options for managing your GERD or LPR. It's crucial to be mindful of your beverage choices as much as your food. Starting your day with a reflux-friendly beverage can set the tone for your entire day, ensuring you avoid unnecessary discomfort from the get-go.

First, let's start with what you should avoid. The usual suspects here are caffeine and alcohol, both of which can relax the lower esophageal sphincter (LES), allowing stomach acid to escape back up the esophagus, causing discomfort. Citrus juices, like orange and grapefruit juice, are also high in acid and can exacerbate symptoms. Some people may find that carbonated beverages can also trigger acid reflux.

Now that you know what to dodge, let's look at some options that are good for you.

1. Herbal Teas: these are a comforting, warming alternative to regular tea and coffee. Chamomile and licorice teas are known to be gentle on the stomach and can help reduce inflammation. Ginger tea can also aid digestion and alleviate symptoms of acid reflux.

2. Aloe Vera Juice: yes, the same plant that soothes sunburn can also soothe your esophagus. Aloe vera juice, about 2 oz in the morning, can help reduce stomach and esophagic inflammation.

3. Water with a Dash of Apple Cider Vinegar: although it may sound counterintuitive, apple cider vinegar can actually help some people with acid reflux. Try adding 1-2 tablespoons of apple cider vinegar to 8 oz of water in the morning.

4. Almond Milk: this is an excellent alternative to cow's milk, which can cause some people to produce excess stomach acid. Almond milk is alkaline, so it can help neutralize stomach acid, making it an excellent choice for a morning smoothie base.

5. Green Drinks: blending a mix of green vegetables like spinach, kale, cucumber, and celery can make for a power-packed, low-acid start to the day.

6. Coconut Water: this beverage is naturally high in electrolytes, which can help keep you hydrated and promote a balanced pH in your body.

7. Bone Broth: sipping on bone broth, made from simmering bones and connective tissues of chicken or beef, can be soothing for the digestive system. Plus, it's packed with beneficial collagen and nutrients.

8. Fennel Tea: this mildly sweet, licorice-like flavored tea is an excellent option for acid reflux sufferers. Fennel is known for its stomach-soothing properties and can aid digestion while reducing inflammation in your gastrointestinal tract. To make this at home, simply steep about one tablespoon of fennel seeds in 8 oz of boiling water for 10 minutes, strain, and enjoy.

9. Non-Citrus Juices: while citrus juices are typically a no-go for people with GERD and LPR, many other types of fruit juices can be enjoyed without triggering symptoms. Try juices made from non-citrus fruits like apples, pears, or melons. You could also consider juicing vegetables like carrots or beets. Just make sure to avoid adding any high-acid fruits to the mix.

10. Turmeric Latte: also known as "golden milk," this drink combines dairy-free milk (like almond or coconut milk), turmeric, and a touch of honey for sweetness. Turmeric is known for its anti-inflammatory properties, which can be beneficial for people dealing with digestive issues. Just simmer about a teaspoon of turmeric in 8 oz of your preferred milk, stir in honey to taste, and allow to cool a bit before drinking.

The above drinks are generally considered safe if you're dealing with GERD or LPR, but remember that everyone's body is different. What works well for one person might not work as well for another. If any of these suggestions still trigger your symptoms, it's best to avoid them. The key is to experiment and pay attention to how your body reacts. By choosing suitable beverages, you're taking another step in managing your GERD and LPR symptoms and towards enjoying your mornings with greater ease and comfort.

CHAPTER 4: SATISFYING LUNCH IDEAS

Navigating lunch can sometimes be challenging, especially when dealing with acid reflux, GERD, or LPR. However, you can enjoy a satisfying and delicious lunch respecting your digestive health. The key lies in balancing the meal composition and ensuring it's light and digestible.

A balanced lunch incorporates a variety of food groups to provide you with all the necessary nutrients. Think of this as your middle-of-the-day energy boost that fuels you without overwhelming your stomach. Each component plays a significant role in managing reflux symptoms.

Begin with lean proteins. They are essential for muscle repair and recovery and are a great source of sustained energy throughout the day. Opt for foods like grilled chicken, turkey, or fish. Tofu or legumes can be a good choice if you follow a plant-based diet. However, remember that preparation is key. Aim to grill, steam, or bake instead of frying, as high-fat foods can exacerbate reflux symptoms.

Include a wide array of vegetables. They are full of essential vitamins, minerals, and fibers that help your body function optimally. Fibers are particularly beneficial as they aid digestion and make you feel full for longer, preventing overeating. Favor alkaline vegetables, such as broccoli, cucumbers, and leafy greens, which can help neutralize stomach acids.

Incorporate complex carbohydrates, like whole grains, brown rice, or sweet potatoes. They provide slow-release energy, preventing a sudden spike and blood sugar drop. They also tend to be high in fiber, promoting a healthy digestive system.

Dairy can be tricky for reflux sufferers as it tends to be high in fat, which can trigger symptoms. But not all dairy is created equal. Lower-fat options like mozzarella or feta cheese can often be enjoyed in small amounts. You can also explore dairy-free alternatives such as almond milk or coconut yogurt.

Keep portion sizes in check. A big meal can put pressure on the lower esophageal sphincter (LES), making acid reflux more likely. Aim for a light lunch, enough to satisfy your hunger without feeling too full. Use your hands as a rough guide: a fist-sized portion of carbs, a palm-sized amount of protein, and plenty of vegetables should do the trick.

Last, but not least, be mindful of when you eat. Eating too quickly can lead to overeating and exacerbate acid reflux symptoms. Take the time to savor your meal, chew your food thoroughly, and listen to your body's satiety cues. Also, try to have your lunch at least two to three hours before lying down to prevent the backflow of stomach acid.

Adopting a balanced, light lunch routine may require some adjustments at first. But with time, you'll find that it not only helps manage your reflux symptoms but also contributes to your overall well-being and energy levels throughout the day. It's another step towards a healthier, more enjoyable eating experience. After all, managing GERD and LPR is not just about what you avoid, but also about celebrating what you can enjoy.

Soup recipes

Soup has a comforting and soothing appeal that makes it an excellent choice for lunch, especially when dealing with conditions like GERD and LPR. Soup recipes can be versatile, nourishing, and easily adapted to be reflux-friendly. Let's explore some easy-to-make, stomach-friendly soup recipes.

1. Ginger Carrot Soup

This soup combines the sweetness of carrots with the zest of ginger, known for its anti-inflammatory properties.

Ingredients:

16 oz of carrots (peeled and chopped)
1-inch piece of ginger (peeled and grated)
1 tbsp olive oil
4 cups low-sodium vegetable broth
Salt and pepper to taste

Start by heating the olive oil in a pot over medium heat. Add the carrots and ginger, and cook until the carrots are tender. Pour in the vegetable broth, and bring the mixture to a boil. Reduce the heat and let it simmer until the carrots are fully cooked. Allow the soup to cool slightly, and then blend until smooth. Add salt and pepper to taste, and your Ginger Carrot Soup is ready to serve!

2. Creamy Zucchini Soup:

A light and creamy soup that brings out the delicate flavor of zucchini.

Ingredients:

32 oz of zucchini (chopped)
1 onion (chopped)
2 garlic cloves (minced)
1 tbsp olive oil
4 cups low-sodium chicken broth
Salt and pepper to taste

In a large pot, heat the olive oil and add the onion and garlic. Sauté until they're soft and fragrant. Add the chopped zucchini, and continue to cook until it's tender. Pour in the chicken broth and bring the mixture to a boil. Once boiling, reduce the heat and simmer until the zucchini is fully cooked. After the soup has cooled slightly, blend until smooth. Season with salt and pepper to taste, and enjoy your Creamy Zucchini Soup.

3. Butternut Squash and Pear Soup

This recipe brings a sweet twist to your traditional butternut squash soup, perfect for a refreshing, light lunch.

Ingredients:

1 medium butternut squash (peeled and chopped)
2 ripe pears (peeled and chopped)
1 onion (chopped)
2 cloves of garlic (minced)
1 tbsp olive oil

4 cups low-sodium vegetable broth
Salt and pepper to taste

Heat the olive oil in a pot and add the onion and garlic. Sauté until they're soft. Next, add the butternut squash and pears, and cook until they're tender. Pour in the vegetable broth and bring the mixture to a boil. Reduce the heat and simmer until the squash and pears are fully cooked. Once the soup has cooled slightly, blend until smooth. Add salt and pepper to taste, and your Butternut Squash and Pear Soup is ready to serve!

4. Chicken and Rice Soup

A comforting and filling soup with tender chicken and hearty rice.

Ingredients:

16 oz chicken breast
1 cup long-grain brown rice
1 onion (chopped)
1 tbsp olive oil
4 cups low-sodium chicken broth
Salt and pepper to taste

Start by heating the olive oil in a pot over medium heat. Add the onion and cook until soft. Add the chicken breast and cook until it's no longer pink. Add the chicken broth and bring to a boil. Stir in the rice, reduce the heat, cover, and simmer until the rice is cooked. Season with salt and pepper to taste.

5. Sweet Potato and Leek Soup

This soup is packed with healthy nutrients and has a subtly sweet flavor.

Ingredients:

2 sweet potatoes (peeled and chopped)
2 leeks (washed and sliced)
1 tbsp olive oil
4 cups low-sodium vegetable broth

Salt and pepper to taste

Heat the olive oil in a pot and add the leeks. Cook until soft. Add the sweet potatoes and broth, bring to a boil, then reduce the heat and simmer until the sweet potatoes are soft. Blend the soup until smooth and season with salt and pepper to taste.

6. Cauliflower and Garlic Soup

A creamy soup that's low in acid and high in flavor.

Ingredients:

1 head of cauliflower (chopped)
2 cloves of garlic (minced)
1 tbsp olive oil
4 cups low-sodium vegetable broth
Salt and pepper to taste

In a pot, heat the olive oil and add the garlic. Cook until fragrant. Add the cauliflower and broth, bring to a boil, then simmer until the cauliflower is soft. Blend the soup until smooth and season with salt and pepper to taste.

7. Barley and Mushroom Soup

A hearty soup with a rich, earthy flavor.

Ingredients:

1 cup pearl barley
16 oz mushrooms (sliced)
1 onion (chopped)
1 tbsp olive oil
4 cups low-sodium vegetable broth
Salt and pepper to taste

Heat the olive oil in a pot and add the onion. Cook until soft. Add the mushrooms and cook until they release their liquid. Add the barley and broth, bring to a boil, then reduce the heat and simmer until the barley is tender. Season with salt and pepper to taste.

8. Tomato and Basil Soup

A classic soup that's light and flavorful.

Ingredients:

4 cups low-acidity canned tomatoes
1 cup fresh basil leaves
1 onion (chopped)
1 tbsp olive oil
4 cups low-sodium vegetable broth
Salt and pepper to taste

In a pot, heat the olive oil and add the onion. Cook until soft. Add the tomatoes, broth, and half of the basil. Bring to a boil, then simmer for 15 minutes. Add the rest of the basil, blend until smooth, and season with salt and pepper to taste.

9. Spinach and White Bean Soup

A hearty soup packed with fiber and protein.

Ingredients:

16 oz spinach leaves
1 can white beans (rinsed and drained)
1 onion (chopped)
1 tbsp olive oil
4 cups low-sodium vegetable broth
Salt and pepper to taste

Heat the olive oil in a pot and add the onion. Cook until soft. Add the spinach and cook until wilted. Add the beans and broth, bring to a boil, then simmer for 15 minutes. Blend the soup until smooth and season with salt and pepper to taste.

10. Broccoli and Cheddar Soup:

A creamy and delicious soup that's also good for you.

Ingredients:

1 head of broccoli (chopped)
1 cup low-fat cheddar cheese
1 onion (chopped)
1 tbsp olive oil
4 cups low-sodium vegetable broth
Salt and pepper to taste

In a pot, heat the olive oil and add the onion. Cook until soft. Add the broccoli and broth, bring to a boil, then simmer until the broccoli is soft. Turn off the heat and stir in the cheese until melted. Blend the soup until smooth and season with salt and pepper to taste.

Remember, these recipes are only a starting point. Feel free to adjust them to suit your tastes and preferences. The most crucial aspect is ensuring the ingredients are fresh and GERD and LPR-friendly. Enjoy the process of creating, and most importantly, savor the result, knowing that you are nourishing your body and caring for your digestive health.

Salads with reflux-friendly dressings

Salads are an excellent choice for a light and refreshing lunch that won't trigger your GERD or LPR symptoms. While choosing the right ingredients is essential, it's equally important to dress your salad in a way that complements the elements without introducing excess acidity or fat. Here are several salad recipes with reflux-friendly dressings you can incorporate into your lunch rotation.

1. Chicken Avocado Salad with Lemon Vinaigrette

This salad provides a good balance of protein and healthy fats, both of which help to maintain a feeling of fullness without causing reflux.

Ingredients:

6 oz grilled chicken breast (sliced)
1 ripe avocado (sliced)
2 cups of mixed greens
For the vinaigrette: 2 tbsp fresh lemon juice, 1/2 cup olive oil, salt and pepper to taste.

Start by mixing the ingredients for the vinaigrette in a bowl. Place the mixed greens on a plate, top with the sliced chicken and avocado, and drizzle with the vinaigrette.

2. Quinoa and Vegetable Salad with Cilantro Lime Dressing

Quinoa is a complete protein and a great source of fiber. Combined with various colorful vegetables, it makes for a filling and nutrient-rich salad.

Ingredients:

1 cup cooked quinoa
1 cup chopped cucumber
1 cup cherry tomatoes (halved)
1 cup bell pepper (chopped)
For the dressing: 1/4 cup fresh lime juice, 1/2 cup olive oil, 1/4 cup chopped cilantro, salt and pepper to taste.

Combine the quinoa and vegetables in a large bowl. Mix the dressing ingredients in a separate bowl, then pour over the salad and mix well.

3. Chickpea and Feta Salad with Mint Yogurt Dressing

The chickpeas in this salad offer a great source of protein and fiber, while the feta adds a tangy flavor that doesn't have the fat content of heavier cheeses.

Ingredients:

1 can chickpeas (rinsed and drained)
1 cup cherry tomatoes (halved)

1/2 cup crumbled feta cheese
For the dressing: 1/2 cup plain Greek yogurt, 1/4 cup chopped fresh mint, 2 tbsp olive oil, salt and pepper to taste.

In a large bowl, combine the chickpeas, tomatoes, and feta. Whisk together the dressing ingredients in a separate bowl and pour over the salad. Toss to combine.

4. Beetroot and Spinach Salad with Ginger Dressing

This recipe features nutrient-rich beetroot and spinach, with a refreshing ginger dressing to add zing.

Ingredients:

2 cups fresh spinach
1 medium beetroot (cooked and sliced)
1/4 cup walnuts
For the dressing: 1 tbsp grated ginger, 3 tbsp olive oil, 1 tbsp apple cider vinegar, salt and pepper to taste.

Layer the spinach, beetroot, and walnuts on a plate. Whisk together the dressing ingredients and drizzle over the salad.

5. Broccoli and Cauliflower Salad with Tahini Dressing

A delicious cruciferous mix, this salad is high in fiber and pairs perfectly with a creamy, nutty tahini dressing.

Ingredients:

2 cups broccoli florets (steamed)
2 cups cauliflower florets (steamed)
1/4 cup sunflower seeds
For the dressing: 2 tbsp tahini, 2 tbsp lemon juice, 2 tbsp olive oil, salt and pepper to taste.

Combine the broccoli, cauliflower, and sunflower seeds in a bowl. Mix the dressing ingredients and pour over the salad, tossing to coat.

6. Tuna and White Bean Salad with Dill Dressing

This protein-packed salad is ideal for a post-workout lunch.

Ingredients:

1 can tuna in water (drained)
1 can white beans (rinsed and drained)
1/2 cup chopped cucumber
For the dressing: 1/4 cup fresh dill (chopped), 1/4 cup olive oil, 1 tbsp white wine vinegar, salt and pepper to taste.

Mix the tuna, beans, and cucumber in a bowl. Stir together the dressing ingredients and toss through the salad.

7. Grilled Veggie and Quinoa Salad with Basil Vinaigrette

Grilled vegetables offer a rich, smoky flavor that pairs well with earthy quinoa.

Ingredients:

1 cup cooked quinoa
2 cups mixed grilled vegetables (zucchini, bell peppers, eggplant)
For the dressing: 1/4 cup fresh basil leaves, 1/4 cup olive oil, 1 tbsp apple cider vinegar, salt and pepper to taste.

Mix the quinoa and vegetables in a bowl. Blend the dressing ingredients until smooth and drizzle over the salad.

8. Lentil and Avocado Salad with Cumin Lime Dressing

This filling salad features fiber-rich lentils and creamy avocado.

Ingredients:

1 cup cooked lentils
1 ripe avocado (sliced)
2 cups mixed salad greens
For the dressing: 1 tsp ground cumin, 2 tbsp lime juice, 1/4 cup olive oil, salt and pepper to taste.

Combine the lentils, avocado, and salad greens in a bowl. Mix the dressing ingredients and toss through the salad.

9. Roasted Pumpkin and Kale Salad with Lemon Garlic Dressing

The sweetness of roasted pumpkin contrasts beautifully with peppery kale in this salad.

Ingredients:

2 cups cubed pumpkin (roasted)
2 cups kale (chopped)
1/4 cup pumpkin seeds
For the dressing: 2 tbsp lemon juice, 1 clove garlic (minced), 1/4 cup olive oil, salt and pepper to taste.

Combine the pumpkin, kale, and pumpkin seeds in a bowl. Whisk together the dressing ingredients and pour over the salad, tossing to coat.

10. Mango and Black Bean Salad with Coriander Lime Dressing

This tropical salad is bursting with color and flavor.

Ingredients:

1 ripe mango (cubed)
1 can black beans (rinsed and drained)
1/2 cup red bell pepper (diced)
For the dressing: 1/4 cup fresh coriander (chopped), 2 tbsp lime juice, 1/4 cup olive oil, salt and pepper to taste.

Mix the mango, beans, and bell pepper in a bowl. Stir together the dressing ingredients and pour over the salad, tossing to combine.

These salad recipes demonstrate that you can enjoy a wide variety of flavors while adhering to a diet that minimizes acid reflux and LPR symptoms. Remember, the key to keeping your salads GERD and LPR-friendly is to use fresh, lean ingredients and dressings that are low in fat and acidity. So feel free to experiment and find combinations that you enjoy, and that also make you feel your best. Eating healthily doesn't mean missing out on flavor or variety. It's all about making intelligent choices that suit your individual needs and tastes.

Wraps

Wraps are a wonderful lunch choice, being portable, versatile, and, most importantly, adaptable to the dietary needs of people managing GERD and LPR. Let's explore some delicious and reflux-friendly wrap recipes you can quickly whip up for lunch.

1. Grilled Chicken & Avocado Wrap

Ingredients:

4 oz grilled chicken breast, sliced
1/2 ripe avocado, thinly sliced
1 cup fresh spinach
1/2 cucumber, julienned
1 whole grain wrap
1 tbsp low-fat Greek yogurt
Fresh herbs: basil, cilantro (as tolerated)

Spread the Greek yogurt on the wrap, then pile on the spinach, cucumber, chicken, and avocado. Add some fresh herbs, roll the wrap, and enjoy. Chicken is a lean protein, great for GERD, and avocado offers healthy fats.

2. Hummus & Veggie Wrap

Ingredients:
2 tbsp hummus
1 whole grain wrap
A selection of fresh veggies: bell pepper, carrots, lettuce
1/4 cup chickpeas, cooked
Fresh parsley, chopped

Spread the hummus on the wrap, add a hefty serving of veggies, sprinkle some chickpeas, garnish with fresh parsley, and wrap it up. This wrap is plant-based and full of fiber, which is crucial for maintaining good digestive health.

3. Turkey & Swiss Chard Wrap

Ingredients:

4 oz turkey breast, sliced
1 whole grain wrap
Swiss chard leaves, chopped
1 small carrot, grated
1 tbsp mustard
1/2 apple, thinly sliced

Lay the wrap flat and spread a thin layer of mustard on it. Then add the Swiss chard leaves, turkey slices, grated carrot, and apple slices. Roll it up for a satisfying lunch. Turkey is another lean protein, while apples provide a sweet crunch without triggering reflux.

4. Tofu & Veggie Wrap

Ingredients:

4 oz tofu, grilled and sliced
1/2 cup mixed greens
Sliced cucumber and bell peppers
1 whole grain wrap
1 tbsp tahini

Spread tahini on the wrap, then add the mixed greens, veggies, and tofu slices. Roll it up and enjoy a protein-rich, vegetarian lunch.

5. Quinoa & Avocado Wrap

Ingredients:

1/2 cup cooked quinoa
1/2 avocado, sliced
1/2 cup chopped lettuce
1 whole grain wrap

Spread the cooked quinoa on the wrap, top with avocado slices and lettuce, then roll it up. This fiber-filled wrap is easy to digest and packed with nutrients.

6. Greek-Style Wrap

Ingredients:

4 oz grilled chicken breast, sliced
1/2 cup chopped cucumber
1/2 tomato, chopped
Fresh parsley, chopped
1 whole grain wrap
1 tbsp low-fat Greek yogurt

Spread the Greek yogurt on the wrap, add the chicken, cucumber, and tomato, garnish with fresh parsley, and roll it up for a Mediterranean-inspired lunch.

7. Salmon & Greens Wrap

Ingredients:

4 oz grilled salmon
1 cup spinach leaves
1/2 cucumber, sliced

1 whole grain wrap
1 tbsp low-fat cream cheese

Spread cream cheese on the wrap, then add the spinach, cucumber, and grilled salmon. Roll it up for a delicious source of lean protein and omega-3 fatty acids.

8. Egg Salad Wrap

Ingredients:

2 hard-boiled eggs, chopped
1/4 avocado, mashed
1/2 cup lettuce
1 whole grain wrap

Mix the chopped eggs and mashed avocado to make a healthy egg salad. Spread it on the wrap, top it with lettuce, and roll it up for a protein-rich, reflux-friendly lunch.

9. Lentil & Veggie Wrap

Ingredients:

1/2 cup cooked lentils
A mix of sliced veggies: bell pepper, cucumber, lettuce
1 whole grain wrap

Spread the cooked lentils on the wrap, top with the sliced veggies, and roll it up. This plant-based wrap is high in fiber and nutrients.

10. Shrimp & Cabbage Wrap

Ingredients:

4 oz cooked shrimp
1/2 cup shredded cabbage
1/2 carrot, grated

Fresh cilantro, chopped
1 whole grain wrap
1 tbsp low-fat mayo

Spread the mayo on the wrap, then add the cabbage, carrot, shrimp, and garnish with fresh cilantro. Roll it up for a delicious, ocean-inspired lunch.

Remember to listen to your body. If certain ingredients trigger your reflux, don't hesitate to replace or remove them from these recipes. The goal is to enjoy your meals while managing your symptoms. It's not about a strict list of dos and don'ts but about creating a sustainable, enjoyable, and healthful eating routine that suits your body and lifestyle. Wraps offer a convenient and versatile option that can be tailored to your tastes while keeping your symptoms at bay. So go ahead and roll up a delicious, nutritious, and reflux-friendly lunch!

Defining the right portion size for your lunch meals can significantly impact managing your acid reflux symptoms. It matters because overeating or eating large meals can put excess pressure on your lower esophageal sphincter, making it easier for stomach acids to splash back up into your esophagus. By limiting your portion sizes, you can help reduce this pressure, thereby reducing your acid reflux symptoms.

It's easy to imagine that your stomach is the size of your clenched fist. Generally, it's good to aim to fill your stomach to about 80% capacity during meals, which helps avoid overeating. That means you should feel satisfied, but not overly stuffed or bloated after a meal. So, how can you achieve that?

Start with your protein source, whether it be animal-based, like chicken, fish, or eggs, or plant-based, like tofu or legumes. A proper portion size of cooked meat, poultry, or fish is typically around 3 to 4 oz, which is roughly the size of a deck of cards. For cooked legumes or tofu, aim for about 1/2 cup.

Next, look at your grain-based foods. A serving of whole grain bread, wrap, or pasta is typically about 1 oz, while a serving of cooked grains like brown rice or quinoa is about 1/2 cup. As a visual guide, that's approximately the size of your cupped hand.

Now, let's move on to fruits and vegetables. When it comes to veggies, you can be a bit more generous. Aim for at least 1 cup of raw, leafy greens or 1/2 cup of other cooked or raw veggies. If you add fruit to your lunch meal, a serving is usually about 1/2 cup of chopped fruit or a small piece of whole fruit.

Don't forget about fats. While beneficial, healthy fats like avocado, nuts, and seeds are high in calories and should be eaten in moderation. A serving size is typically about 1 tablespoon for oils, 2 tablespoons for nut butter, 1/4 of an avocado, or a small handful of nuts or seeds.

Lastly, if your lunch includes dairy or an alternative, a serving size is generally 1 cup for milk or yogurt or 1.5 oz for cheese.

While these are general guidelines, remember that everyone's needs are different. Depending on factors such as your size, age, sex, activity level, and overall health, you may require more or less food. It's essential to listen to your body's hunger and fullness cues and adjust your portion sizes accordingly.

Also, you might find it helpful to eat smaller, more frequent meals rather than three large ones each day. This approach can help prevent your stomach from becoming too full and triggering reflux symptoms. For example, you might eat a small lunch, followed by a mid-afternoon snack, instead of a larger, more substantial lunch.

In addition, take your time when you eat. Try to make your meal last at least 20-30 minutes, as it takes about 20 minutes for your brain to register that you're full. By slowing down, you're less likely to overeat and more likely to enjoy your meal.

Managing acid reflux isn't just about what you eat; it's also about how much you eat. By being mindful of your portion sizes, you can help keep your symptoms in check while enjoying a varied and nutritious diet.

CHAPTER 5: MOUTHWATERING DINNER DELIGHT

In managing GERD and LPR, dinner holds unique importance. The last meal of the day provides the essential nutrients to fuel your body throughout the night. A comforting, satisfying dinner helps you end the day positively and prepares you for a restful night's sleep.

The first aspect to consider is the timing of dinner. Eating at least three hours before bed gives your body ample time to digest food, thereby reducing the likelihood of experiencing nighttime acid reflux. Your lower esophageal sphincter, the muscle that keeps stomach acid from backing up into your esophagus, functions best when it's not contending with a full stomach. By giving yourself a few hours between eating and lying down, you allow it to do its job more efficiently.

While the timing is crucial, so is the content of your meal. A satisfying dinner should contain balanced proportions of lean protein, whole grains, and vegetables. You may be tempted to skip carbohydrates or eat a very light meal, but it's important to remember that balance is key. Whole grains like brown rice, quinoa, and whole wheat pasta provide slow-releasing energy to keep you satisfied throughout the night. Lean proteins, such as fish, poultry, and tofu, contribute essential amino acids for repairing and rebuilding body tissues. Finally, colorful vegetables add vital vitamins, minerals, and fiber, promoting overall health.

But satisfaction isn't just about physical fullness; it's also about enjoyment. Don't neglect the flavors you love in your quest for reflux-friendly meals. While it's true that certain foods can trigger acid reflux, such as spicy foods, high-fat foods, citrus fruits, and tomatoes, it doesn't mean your dinner has to be bland and boring. Experiment with various herbs, spices, and cooking techniques to create dishes that excite your palate and satisfy your cravings. For example, roasting vegetables brings out their natural sweetness, and marinating proteins can add depth and complexity of flavor without the need for trigger foods.

Creating a comfortable eating environment is another aspect of a comforting dinner. Stress can worsen GERD and LPR symptoms, so making your mealtime a peaceful, relaxing experience is beneficial. This could mean turning off distracting electronic devices, lighting candles, playing calming music, or simply ensuring your dining area is clean and inviting.

Lastly, portion control is essential, even at dinner. Despite the temptation to have a large meal at the end of the day, overeating can put extra pressure on your lower esophageal sphincter and lead to acid reflux. Stick to the portion size guidelines discussed earlier and listen to your body's hunger and fullness cues.

In conclusion, a comforting, satisfying dinner plays an integral role in managing GERD and LPR. By paying attention to meal timing, maintaining a balanced diet, incorporating enjoyable flavors, creating a relaxing dining atmosphere, and observing portion control, you can ensure your dinner works for you, not against you, in your journey towards a reflux-free life.

One-pot meal recipes

There's something genuinely satisfying about creating a delicious, well-balanced meal that only uses one pot. Not only does it mean less cleanup, but it also offers a fantastic opportunity to allow flavors to meld together beautifully. So, let's explore a collection of one-pot meals that are easy to prepare, delicious, and, most importantly, won't exacerbate your GERD or LPR symptoms.

1. Quinoa Primavera

This delightful dish combines the light fluffiness of quinoa with the fresh taste of bell peppers, zucchini, and carrots, all sautéed to perfection and served with a hint of your favorite fresh herbs.

Ingredients:

1 cup of quinoa
2 cups of low-sodium chicken broth
1 bell pepper (diced)

1 zucchini (diced)
2 carrots (diced)
Olive oil
Salt and pepper
Fresh basil and parsley for garnish

Rinse the quinoa under cold water before cooking. In a pot, combine quinoa with broth, bring to a boil, then reduce the heat and let it simmer until the quinoa is tender and fluffy. Meanwhile, sauté the diced vegetables in a bit of olive oil until they're tender. Once everything is cooked, combine the vegetables and quinoa, seasoning with salt and pepper to your liking. Garnish with fresh basil and parsley for an added burst of flavor.

2. Chicken and Brown Rice Casserole

This heartening casserole brings together tender chicken and wholesome brown rice, all beautifully seasoned and garnished with fresh parsley.

Ingredients:

Boneless
Skinless chicken breasts
Salt
Pepper
Paprika
Olive oil
1 cup of brown rice
2 cups of low-sodium chicken broth
Fresh parsley for garnish

Season your chicken breasts with salt, pepper, and paprika. Heat some olive oil in a pot and sear the chicken until it's browned on both sides. Remove the chicken and set aside. In the same pot, add your brown rice and broth. Place the seared chicken on top, cover the pot, and let it simmer until the rice is tender and the chicken is thoroughly cooked. Once cooked, garnish with freshly chopped parsley.

3. Lentil and Veggie Stew

A hearty, nourishing stew that's packed with protein-rich lentils and a medley of delicious veggies, finished with a squeeze of fresh lemon juice.

Ingredients:
1 diced onion
2 diced carrots
2 diced celery stalks
Olive oil
1 cup of lentils
4 cups of vegetable broth
A handful of baby spinach
Fresh lemon juice

Start by sautéing your diced onion, carrots, and celery stalks in a bit of olive oil in a large pot. Once the vegetables have softened, add in the lentils and vegetable broth, allowing everything to simmer until the lentils become tender. Near the end of the cooking time, stir in a handful of baby spinach until it wilts, then finish everything off with a squeeze of fresh lemon juice for a bright, zesty kick.

4. Shrimp and Farro Paella

A simple yet flavorful dish that combines the nutty flavor of farro with succulent shrimp and colorful vegetables, all brought together with a sprinkling of fresh parsley.

Ingredients:

1 sliced bell pepper
1 sliced onion
Olive oil
1 cup of farro
2 cups of low-sodium chicken broth
Peeled and deveined shrimp
Fresh parsley for garnish

Heat some olive oil in a pot and sauté the sliced bell pepper and onion until softening. Stir in the farro, then pour in the broth. Allow this to simmer until the farro is nearly cooked, at which point you can add in the shrimp. Continue to cook until the shrimp are pink and opaque, then garnish the whole dish with a sprinkle of freshly chopped parsley.

5. Veggie-Packed Frittata

A versatile dish that is perfect for using up any leftover veggies. The eggs provide a good source of protein, keeping you satiated for longer.

Ingredients:

6 large eggs
2 cups of your favorite low-acid veggies (e.g., zucchini, bell peppers, spinach)
Olive oil
Salt
Pepper

Preheat your oven to 375°F. In an oven-safe skillet, sauté your chosen veggies in olive oil until they are tender. Whisk together the eggs, salt, and pepper in a separate bowl. Pour this mixture over your sautéed veggies and let it cook until the edges start to pull away from the pan. Transfer the skillet to your preheated oven and bake until the eggs are set, about 10-12 minutes.

6. Sweet Potato and Black Bean Chili

This recipe combines sweet potatoes' natural sweetness with hearty black beans in a satisfying, flavorful chili.

Ingredients:

1 diced sweet potato
1 can of black beans (drained and rinsed)
1 diced onion
2 cups of vegetable broth
Olive oil
Chili powder

Cumin

In a pot, sauté your diced onion in olive oil until it's translucent. Add the diced sweet potato and spices, stirring until the sweet potato is coated. Pour in your vegetable broth and black beans, then simmer until the sweet potato is tender. Adjust seasonings to taste.

7. Baked Salmon with Quinoa and Broccoli

This is a lean, protein-rich dish that's full of flavor and omega-3 fatty acids.

Ingredients:

4 salmon fillets
1 cup of quinoa
2 cups of vegetable broth
1 head of broccoli (cut into florets)
Olive oil
Salt
Pepper

Preheat your oven to 400°F. Season the salmon with salt and pepper and place it in a large baking dish. Around the salmon, add the quinoa, broccoli, and vegetable broth. Drizzle everything with a bit of olive oil, then cover the dish with foil and bake until the quinoa is tender and the salmon is cooked through, about 20-25 minutes.

8. Ginger Garlic Chicken Stir Fry

This stir-fry has a robust flavor profile with ginger and garlic, plus a colorful array of veggies.

Ingredients:

Boneless
Skinless chicken breasts (cut into thin strips)
3 cups of your favorite stir-fry veggies (e.g., bell peppers, bok choy, carrots)

Olive oil
Minced ginger
Minced garlic
Low-sodium soy sauce

Heat a bit of olive oil in a wok or large pan, then add your chicken strips, cooking until they're no longer pink. Remove the chicken and set it aside. Add a bit more olive oil in the same pan, then sauté your veggies until they're tender. Add the minced ginger and garlic, stirring until fragrant, then add the chicken back into the pan. Drizzle everything with a bit of low-sodium soy sauce, tossing to combine.

9. Baked Tofu with Veggies

This dish is perfect for those following a plant-based diet. It's filled with protein-rich tofu and an assortment of colorful veggies.

Ingredients:

1 block of tofu (pressed and cubed)
2 cups of your favorite veggies (like bell peppers, zucchini, and broccoli)
Olive oil
Low-sodium soy sauce

Preheat your oven to 400°F. Arrange the tofu and veggies in a single layer on a baking sheet, then drizzle them with olive oil and soy sauce, tossing to combine. Bake until the veggies are tender, and the tofu is golden, about 20-25 minutes.

10. Turkey and Brown Rice Stuffed Peppers

A satisfying, protein-packed dish that's brimming with flavor.

Ingredients:

4 bell peppers (tops removed and seeded)
16 oz of ground turkey

1 cup of cooked brown rice
1 diced onion
Olive oil
Salt
Pepper

Preheat your oven to 375°F. In a skillet, sauté your diced onion in olive oil until it's translucent, then add the ground turkey, cooking until it's no longer pink. Stir in the cooked brown rice and season with salt and pepper to taste. Stuff this mixture into your prepared bell peppers, then place the peppers in a baking dish. Cover the dish with foil and bake until the peppers are tender, about 30-35 minutes.

Reflux-friendly entrees

Let's dive into some delightful entrees that don't skimp on taste or satisfaction, all while being gentle on your system. These are meals that feel like a celebration at the end of the day, without worsening your GERD or LPR symptoms.

1. Grilled Vegetable Kabobs

Simple and flavorful, these kabobs make a light and refreshing entrée.

Ingredients:

1 bell pepper
1 zucchini
1 red onion
8 cherry tomatoes
Olive oil
Salt
Pepper for seasoning

Preheat your grill or grill pan. Cut the vegetables into chunks, then thread them onto skewers, alternating the vegetables. Brush lightly with olive oil and season with salt and pepper. Grill until charred and tender, about 10-12 minutes, turning occasionally.

2. Baked Sweet Potato Rounds

These sweet potato rounds are a satisfying, fiber-rich entrée that's easy on the stomach.

Ingredients:

2 large sweet potatoes
Olive oil
Salt
Pepper

Preheat your oven to 400°F. Slice the sweet potatoes into 1/2-inch rounds. Arrange on a baking sheet, drizzle with olive oil, and season with salt and pepper. Bake until tender and lightly browned, about 20-25 minutes.

3. Roasted Beet Salad

This colorful salad is a refreshing and easy-to-digest entrée.

Ingredients:

2 medium beets
4 cups mixed salad greens
1/2 cup crumbled feta cheese
For the dressing: 1/4 cup olive oil, 1 tbsp honey, salt, and pepper.

Preheat your oven to 400°F. Wrap the beets in foil and roast until tender, about 60 minutes. Once cool, peel the beets and slice. Arrange the salad greens on plates, top with beet slices and feta, and drizzle with the dressing.

4. Steamed Artichokes

Artichokes are a fun and interactive entrée that's gentle on the stomach.

Ingredients:

2 large artichokes

1 lemon
Salt

Trim the stems and tops of the artichokes. Fill a pot with a few inches of water, add salt, and bring to a boil. Add the artichokes and the juice of the lemon. Cover and steam until the leaves can be easily pulled off, about 45-60 minutes. Serve warm.

5. Cucumber and Dill Yogurt Dip

This refreshing dip is ideally served with whole wheat crackers or raw veggies.

Ingredients:

1 cup plain Greek yogurt
1 small cucumber (seeded and finely chopped)
2 tbsp chopped fresh dill
1 garlic clove (minced)
Salt
Pepper

Mix together the yogurt, cucumber, dill, and garlic. Season with salt and pepper. Chill before serving.

6. Baked Parmesan Zucchini Rounds

This dish showcases zucchini in its most elegant form. The rich, salty Parmesan perfectly complements the light flavors of zucchini.

Ingredients:

2 medium-sized zucchinis
1/2 cup grated Parmesan
Olive oil
Salt to taste

Preheat your oven to 425°F. Slice the zucchinis into 1/4-inch thick rounds. Lay them out on a baking sheet, lightly brush with olive oil and season with salt. Sprinkle the tops with Parmesan and bake for 15-20 minutes, or until the Parmesan turns a golden brown.

7. Roasted Brussels Sprouts

Once roasted, Brussels sprouts become a flavorful, caramelized side dish that even grows skeptics will enjoy. The simple preparation allows the natural flavors of the sprouts to shine.

Ingredients:

16 oz Brussels sprouts halved
2 tablespoons olive oil
Salt
Pepper to taste

Preheat your oven to 400°F. Toss the Brussels sprouts in olive oil, season with salt and pepper, and spread out on a baking sheet. Roast for 20-25 minutes, or until tender and slightly caramelized.

8. Turkey Chili with Sweet Potato

This comforting dish uses sweet potato instead of beans for a lower-acidity chili.

Ingredients:

16 oz lean ground turkey
2 large sweet potatoes (cubed)
1 onion (diced)
2 cups of chicken broth
1 tbsp chili powder
Olive oil
Salt
Pepper

Heat some olive oil in a large pot. Add the turkey and onion, cooking until the turkey is browned and the onion is softened. Add the sweet potatoes, chicken broth, chili powder, salt, and pepper. Bring to a boil, then reduce to a simmer and cover. Cook until the sweet potatoes are tender, and the flavors are melded together, about 20-30 minutes.

9. Tofu Stir-Fry with Brown Rice

A plant-based entrée that's full of different textures and flavors.

Ingredients:

1 block of tofu (pressed and cubed)
2 cups of stir-fry veggies (e.g., bell peppers, carrots, bok choy)
1 cup of brown rice
Olive oil
Low-sodium soy sauce

Cook the brown rice according to package instructions. Meanwhile, heat some olive oil in a large pan or wok. Add the tofu and cook until it's golden on all sides. Add the veggies and stir-fry until they're tender. Drizzle with low-sodium soy sauce. Serve the stir-fry over a portion of brown rice.

10. Sweet Potato and Black Bean Quesadillas

This quesadilla is a unique and flavorful dish. The sweet potato provides a sweet note, while the black beans add heartiness. The result is a satisfying, comforting entree that's great for managing GERD and LPR.

Ingredients:

2 medium sweet potatoes
1 can black beans, rinsed and drained
1/2 teaspoon cumin
1/2 teaspoon chili powder
8 small corn tortillas
1 cup shredded cheddar cheese
Olive oil

Preheat your oven to 400°F. Pierce the sweet potatoes with a fork and bake for 40-50 minutes, until soft. Once cooled, scoop the sweet potato flesh into a bowl and mix with black beans, cumin, and chili powder. Divide the mixture evenly between the tortillas, sprinkle with cheese, and fold in half. Heat a bit of olive oil over medium heat in a large skillet. Cook the quesadillas on each side until golden brown, about 3-4 minutes. Cut into wedges and serve.

11. Herb-Roasted Chicken and Brussels Sprouts

This wholesome dish uses the power of herbs for flavor without relying on acidity or spice.

Ingredients:

4 chicken breasts (around 6 oz each)
16 oz Brussels sprouts (halved)
Olive oil
1 tsp dried thyme
1 tsp dried rosemary
Salt
Pepper

Preheat your oven to 400°F. Toss the Brussels sprouts in olive oil, half of the herbs, salt, and pepper, and spread them out on a baking sheet. Nestle the chicken breasts among the sprouts and season them with the remaining herbs, salt, and pepper. Roast until the chicken reaches an internal temperature of 165°F and the sprouts, are tender and caramelized, about 25-30 minutes.

12. Baked Tilapia with Couscous and Steamed Zucchini

This dish is light yet satisfying, with a lean fish and high-fiber sides.

Ingredients:

4 tilapia fillets (around 6 oz each)
1 cup couscous
2 zucchinis (sliced into half-moons)
Olive oil

Salt
Pepper

Preheat your oven to 400°F. Arrange the tilapia on a baking sheet, drizzle with olive oil, and season with salt and pepper. Bake until the fish flakes easily with a fork, about 10-12 minutes. Meanwhile, cook the couscous according to package instructions and steam the zucchini until it's tender. Serve each fillet with a portion of couscous and zucchini.

13. Baked Salmon with Quinoa and Roasted Asparagus

This omega-3-rich dish is as good for your heart as it is for your stomach.

Ingredients:

4 salmon fillets (around 6 oz each)
1 cup quinoa
1 bunch of asparagus (ends trimmed)
Olive oil
Salt
Pepper

Preheat your oven to 400°F. Arrange the salmon and asparagus on a baking sheet, drizzle with olive oil, and season with salt and pepper. Bake until the salmon flakes easily with a fork and the asparagus is tender and crisp, about 12-15 minutes. Meanwhile, cook the quinoa according to package instructions. Serve each fillet with a portion of quinoa and asparagus.

14. Grilled Chicken with Quinoa and Steamed Veggies

A balanced, high-protein meal that's easy on the stomach.

Ingredients:

4 chicken breasts (around 6 oz each)
1 cup quinoa
2 cups of your favorite veggies (broccoli, bell peppers, and carrots work well)
Olive oil

Salt
Pepper

First, cook the quinoa according to package instructions, typically in a 2:1 ratio of water to quinoa. Meanwhile, grill the chicken breasts until they reach an internal temperature of 165°F. Steam your vegetables until they're tender yet crisp. Season the chicken and veggies lightly with salt and pepper. Plate up with a serving of quinoa, a chicken breast, and a serving of vegetables.

These entrées are meant to whet your appetite without triggering any reflux symptoms. They are light, easy to digest, and filled with nutrient-rich ingredients to support your overall health while managing GERD and LPR.

Side dishes that complement the main course

Regarding completing your meals, side dishes play a crucial role. They not only fill out your plate but can enhance your main course's flavors while still aligning with a diet for managing GERD and LPR. Side dishes should provide diversity in your meal and make it even more enjoyable without triggering discomfort.

Vegetables are a safe bet when it comes to reflux-friendly side dishes. They're typically low in acid and high in fiber, making them a good choice for those with GERD or LPR. Roasting, steaming, or grilling them are some ways to prepare your veggies that allow their natural flavors to shine through.

1. Lemon-Thyme Roasted Carrots

Sweet, tender, and beautifully roasted, these carrots perfectly accompany any main dish.

Ingredients:

16 oz carrots
1 tablespoon olive oil
1 tablespoon fresh thyme
Zest and juice of 1/2 a lemon
Salt to taste

Preheat your oven to 425°F. Toss the carrots with olive oil, thyme, lemon zest, juice, and salt. Roast for 20-25 minutes, until tender and slightly caramelized.

Quinoa is a grain that's not only high in fiber but also protein, making it a great addition to any meal. Quinoa salads can be versatile and easily customizable based on what you have on hand.

2. Quinoa Salad with Cucumbers and Olives

This Mediterranean-inspired salad combines the nutty flavor of quinoa with the crispness of cucumbers and tangy olives.

Ingredients:

1 cup quinoa
2 cups water
1 cucumber
1/2 cup olives
2 tablespoons olive oil
1 tablespoon lemon juice
Salt to taste

Rinse quinoa under cold water until the water runs clear. Bring the quinoa and water to a boil in a saucepan. Reduce the heat to a simmer and cover, cooking for 15 minutes. Let cool. Toss the cooled quinoa with the cucumber, olives, olive oil, lemon juice, and salt.

Another excellent option for a side dish is a simple, well-dressed salad. They're quick, easy and provide a fresh, crisp counterpoint to your main dish.

3. Mixed Greens with Raspberry Vinaigrette

Fresh and light, this salad will bring a pop of color and flavor to your dinner table.

Ingredients:

5 oz mixed salad greens

1/2 cup fresh raspberries
2 tablespoons olive oil
1 tablespoon white balsamic vinegar
Salt to taste

Toss the salad greens with the raspberries. Whisk together the olive oil, vinegar, and salt in a small bowl. Drizzle the dressing over the salad.

4. Steamed Green Beans with Almonds

Crisp green beans paired with crunchy almonds for a delightful side.

Ingredients:

16 oz green beans
1/4 cup slivered almonds
Salt to taste

Steam the green beans until tender-crisp, about 5 minutes. Toss with the almonds and salt.

5. Cilantro-Lime Brown Rice

This tangy and aromatic rice is the perfect accompaniment for any protein.

Ingredients:

1 cup brown rice
2 cups water
2 tablespoons fresh cilantro
Juice of 1 lime
Salt to taste.

Cook the brown rice according to package instructions. Stir in the cilantro, lime juice, and salt.

6. Zucchini Noodles (Zoodles)

A light and healthy alternative to traditional pasta.

Ingredients:

2 zucchinis
1 tablespoon olive oil
Salt to taste

Spiralize the zucchini into noodles. Sauté in olive oil for 2-3 minutes, until tender. Season with salt.

7. Oven-Roasted Brussels Sprouts

These Brussels sprouts are crispy on the outside, tender on the inside, and flavorful.

Ingredients:

16 oz Brussels sprouts
1 tablespoon olive oil
Salt to taste

Preheat your oven to 400°F. Toss the Brussels sprouts with the olive oil and salt. Roast for 20-25 minutes, until golden and crispy.

8. Garlic Mashed Cauliflower

A lighter take on traditional mashed potatoes.

Ingredients:

1 head cauliflower
2 cloves garlic
1/4 cup unsweetened almond milk
1 tablespoon olive oil
Salt to taste

Steam the cauliflower and garlic until tender. Blend with the almond milk, olive oil, and salt until smooth.

9. Quinoa-Stuffed Bell Peppers

Colorful bell peppers stuffed with protein-packed quinoa.

Ingredients:

4 bell peppers
1 cup quinoa
2 cups water
1/2 cup diced tomatoes
1/4 cup fresh parsley
Salt to taste

Cook the quinoa according to package instructions. Mix in the tomatoes, parsley, and salt. Stuff the bell peppers with the quinoa mixture. Bake at 375°F for 25-30 minutes, until the peppers are tender.

10. Garlic Parmesan Broccoli

Simple and delicious, this side dish is a flavorful way to get your greens.

Ingredients:

16 oz broccoli florets
2 cloves garlic (minced)
2 tablespoons olive oil
2 tablespoons grated Parmesan cheese
Salt to taste

Preheat your oven to 400°F. In a large bowl, combine broccoli, minced garlic, olive oil, and a pinch of salt. Mix until broccoli is well-coated. Spread broccoli out on a baking sheet and roast for 15-20 minutes, until the edges are crispy. Sprinkle with Parmesan cheese before serving.

By choosing side dishes wisely and preparing them in a reflux-friendly manner, you can add variety and excitement to your meals while keeping your symptoms at bay. It's all about balancing flavors, nutrition, and comfort to ensure every dinner brings you not just satisfaction, but also better management of GERD and LPR. And remember, the best side dish is one that you enjoy - so don't be afraid to experiment and find new favorites that suit your tastes and needs.

You know what they say: "Eat breakfast like a king, lunch like a prince, and dinner like a pauper." This saying bears a lot of weight, especially regarding managing acid reflux. Paying close attention to not only what you eat, but also when and how much you eat, can significantly reduce your GERD and LPR symptoms. Let's talk more about this, focusing mainly on your dinner's timing and portion sizes.

First, let's address timing. As someone managing acid reflux, the clock isn't just a measure of time—it's a tool for symptom management. An important rule of thumb is to finish eating at least 3 hours before bed. Lying down too soon after eating can cause the stomach contents to push up against the lower esophageal sphincter, causing or exacerbating acid reflux. By finishing your dinner several hours before bedtime, you allow your body ample time to digest your food, decreasing the likelihood of nocturnal acid reflux.

Moreover, spreading your meals out and eating smaller, more frequent meals rather than one large dinner can also help alleviate symptoms. Overeating at any one meal can cause your stomach to overfill, pushing food upward and increasing the chance of acid reflux.

Now, let's discuss portion sizes. Start by using smaller plates for your meals. By doing so, you can trick your mind into believing that you are eating more than you actually are. It's a psychological trick that helps with portion control, and it's a strategy that dietitians often recommend for weight loss and health maintenance.

A good strategy for managing portion sizes is to use the "plate method." Visualize your plate being divided into quarters. Two-quarters (or half the plate) should be filled with non-starchy vegetables, like leafy greens, broccoli, or bell peppers. One quarter should be dedicated to lean protein sources like chicken, fish, or tofu, and the final quarter should be comprised of complex carbohydrates, such as brown rice, quinoa, or sweet potato.

Also, consider the volume and weight of the foods you eat. Aim for foods that are high in volume but low in calories. Foods like fruits and vegetables, which are high in fiber and water content, can help you feel full without overeating.

Remember to chew your food thoroughly and eat slowly. Digestion begins in the mouth, and by thoroughly chewing your food, you're making it easier for the rest of your digestive system. Eating slowly can help you recognize fullness cues, which can prevent overeating.

By being mindful about your dinner timing and portion sizes, you're not only taking a big step towards managing your acid reflux symptoms, but also paving the way to a healthier lifestyle overall. These guidelines aren't just beneficial for GERD and LPR management—they're generally healthy habits that can improve overall health and well-being.

CHAPTER 6: DELECTABLE SNACKS AND APPETIZERS

On your road to relieving acid reflux symptoms, every bite you take matters. Snacks and appetizers, though often smaller and lighter, play an equally significant role as your main meals. Thoughtfully selected and portioned, these "mini-meals" can help keep acid reflux in check.

It may seem surprising, but snacking can be a boon to managing GERD and LPR symptoms if done correctly. Large meals tend to overfill the stomach, causing a surge in stomach acid and placing pressure on the lower esophageal sphincter. This can lead to acid regurgitation into the esophagus, triggering the familiar discomfort of heartburn. However, consuming smaller, more frequent meals or snacks can prevent the stomach from becoming too full and help keep acid production in check.

So, what's the secret to making snacks and appetizers work for you in managing acid reflux? The key lies in choosing the right foods and paying attention to portion sizes. When it comes to choosing snack foods, your goal should be to opt for those that are less likely to trigger acid reflux. Foods that are low in fat and acid content but high in fiber are ideal choices. Fresh fruits like bananas and apples, raw vegetables such as carrots and cucumbers, whole grain crackers or rice cakes, and lean proteins like turkey slices or hard-boiled eggs are excellent choices. Similarly, hummus, almond butter, or low-fat yogurt can make for GERD-friendly dips and spreads.

It's crucial, too, to be mindful of portion sizes when it comes to snacks and appetizers. Even the healthiest of foods can trigger acid reflux symptoms if eaten in large quantities. An appropriate snack serving might look like a medium-sized piece of fruit, a handful of baby carrots, or a single serving packet of almond butter. The goal here is not to fill up as if you're having a full meal but to tide you over until your next meal.

Appetizers, while typically associated with dining out or entertaining guests, can also be incorporated into your everyday eating plan. Like snack foods, the right appetizers can help curb your hunger without aggravating your GERD or LPR symptoms. Consider starting your dinner with a small salad dressed with a light, vinegar-free dressing or a cup of broth-based vegetable soup. Not only will this help control portion sizes for your main meal, but it can also boost your daily vegetable intake.

The timing of your snacks and appetizers also matters. Rather than reaching for a snack only when you're starving, try to space your snacks and meals evenly throughout the day. This can prevent overeating and reduce the amount of acid your stomach needs to produce.

By being intentional about your snack and appetizer choices, you're not just managing your GERD and LPR symptoms, but also contributing to a balanced and varied diet. It's another way you're taking control, one small bite at a time.

Reflux-friendly snack recipes

Coping with GERD and LPR doesn't mean you need to forego the pleasure of snacking. It's all about the choices you make. With these simple, delicious, and satisfying snack recipes, you can curb your hunger between meals without the worry of triggering discomfort.

1. Baked Banana Chips

Sweet, crispy, and perfectly snackable, these baked banana chips offer an excellent alternative to store-bought versions.

Ingredients:

2 medium bananas
1 tbsp lemon juice

Preheat the oven to 200°F.
Slice the bananas into thin rounds.
Toss the banana slices in the lemon juice to prevent browning.
Arrange them on a baking sheet lined with parchment paper.
Bake for 2-3 hours, flipping halfway through, until they are dry and slightly golden.
Let them cool completely to crisp up.

2. Carrot and Cucumber Sticks with Hummus

These crunchy vegetable sticks paired with creamy hummus offer a satisfying, fiber-rich snack.

Ingredients:

2 medium carrots
1/2 cucumber
2 oz hummus

Cut the carrots and cucumber into sticks.
Serve with hummus on the side for dipping.

3. Apple Almond Delight

This quick and easy snack combines the crunch of apples with protein-rich almond butter.

Ingredients:

1 medium apple
1 tbsp almond butter

Slice the apple into rounds or wedges.
Serve with almond butter for dipping or spreading.

4. Turkey Roll-ups

High in protein and super quick to make, these roll-ups offer a satisfying midday snack.

Ingredients:

4 slices of turkey breast
2 oz low-fat cream cheese
2 large lettuce leaves

Spread the cream cheese evenly onto the turkey slices.
Place a lettuce leaf on top of each slice.
Roll up the turkey slices and cut into bite-sized pieces if desired.

5. Rice Cake and Avocado

A light and crunchy snack rich in healthy fats, perfect for a mid-afternoon pick-me-up.

Ingredients:

1 rice cake
1/4 ripe avocado
Pinch of salt (optional)

Mash the avocado.
Spread the mashed avocado onto the rice cake.
Sprinkle with a pinch of salt if desired.

6. Chia Pudding

This make-ahead, pudding-like snack is both delicious and easy on the stomach.

Ingredients:

2 tbsp chia seeds
1 cup almond milk
1 tsp honey

Mix the chia seeds, almond milk, and honey in a bowl or mason jar.
Let it sit in the fridge for at least two hours, or overnight, until a pudding-like consistency is reached.

7. Oatmeal Raisin Cookies

These homemade cookies are a sweet, satisfying treat that are easy to make and easier on the stomach.

Ingredients:

1/2 cup oats
1/4 cup raisins
1 mashed banana
Pinch of cinnamon

Preheat the oven to 350°F.
Mix the oats, raisins, mashed banana, and cinnamon in a bowl.
Drop spoonfuls onto a lined baking sheet.
Bake for about 15 minutes, or until golden. Let them cool before serving.

8. Baked Zucchini Chips

Crisp and light, these baked zucchini chips are a great option when you want something savory.

Ingredients:

1 large zucchini
1 tablespoon olive oil
Salt to taste

Preheat the oven to 225°F and line a baking sheet with parchment paper.
Slice the zucchini into thin rounds.
Toss the slices in the olive oil and spread them out on the baking sheet.
Bake for about 1.5-2 hours or until crisp, flipping halfway through.
Sprinkle with salt to taste and let cool before enjoying.

9. Pumpkin Seed & Dried Fruit Mix

A simple, portable snack that's full of fiber and healthy fats.

Ingredients:

1 cup raw pumpkin seeds (pepitas)
1/2 cup dried apricots, chopped

1/2 cup raisins

Preheat the oven to 350°F.
Spread the pumpkin seeds on a baking sheet and roast for about 10 minutes, or until golden.
Let the seeds cool before mixing them with the dried apricots and raisins.
Store in an airtight container.

10. Steamed Edamame

A protein-rich snack that's fun to eat and easy on the stomach.

Ingredients:

1 cup frozen edamame in the pod
Salt to taste

Place the edamame in a steamer or in a microwave-safe dish with a bit of water. If using a steamer, steam for 5-10 minutes. If using a microwave, cover the dish with a lid or wrap and microwave for about 2-3 minutes.
Sprinkle with a bit of salt and enjoy warm. The pods aren't edible - squeeze the edamame out of the pod directly into your mouth.

These recipes show that managing acid reflux doesn't limit you to bland, boring foods. It's about making smart choices and being aware of your body's reactions. Enjoy these snacks knowing that you're taking care of your health and delighting your palate at the same time.

Appetizers suitable for guests or parties

Parties and gatherings can be a challenging environment when you're managing acid reflux, but it doesn't have to be so. With some careful selection and a little creativity, you can prepare appetizers that are both pleasing to your guests and gentle on your digestive system.

One of the fundamental principles to remember when planning party appetizers is to steer clear of ingredients known to trigger acid reflux. This includes high-fat foods, spicy dishes, citrus fruits, and heavily tomato-based sauces. By sticking to lean proteins, fruits, vegetables, and whole grains, you can create a variety of enjoyable appetizers. Let's dive into some ideas.

1. Hummus and Veggie Sticks

A refreshing and satisfying appetizer featuring protein-rich hummus paired with an assortment of fresh vegetables.

Ingredients:

2 cups chickpeas
2 cloves garlic
1/2 cup tahini
Juice of 1 lemon
Salt to taste
Assorted vegetables (cucumbers, bell peppers, carrots)

Blend chickpeas, garlic, tahini, lemon juice, and salt in a food processor until smooth.
Slice the vegetables into sticks.
Serve the hummus in a bowl surrounded by the veggie sticks.

2. Chicken Skewers

Flavorful skewers featuring lean chicken and a colorful array of vegetables seasoned with mild herbs and spices.

Ingredients:

2 boneless, skinless chicken breasts
2 bell peppers
1 onion
1 zucchini
1 teaspoon dried oregano
1 teaspoon dried thyme
Salt and black pepper to taste

Cut the chicken and vegetables into chunks.

Thread onto skewers, alternating between chicken and vegetables.
Season with oregano, thyme, salt, and pepper.
Grill until chicken is cooked through and vegetables are tender.

3. Rice Paper Rolls

Light and refreshing rolls filled with fresh vegetables and lean protein, served with a gentle soy or ginger sauce.

Ingredients:

Rice paper rolls
Assorted fresh vegetables
Choice of lean protein (shrimp, chicken)
Herbs (coriander, mint)
Light soy sauce or homemade ginger sauce for dipping

Slice vegetables and proteins into thin strips.
Soak a rice paper roll in warm water until pliable, then lay it flat.
Arrange a small amount of vegetables, protein, and herbs in the center.
Fold in the sides and roll up tightly. Repeat with the remaining rolls.
Serve with the dipping sauce.

4. Baked Salmon Bites

Healthy and delicious bite-sized salmon pieces, lightly seasoned and baked to perfection.

Ingredients:

16 oz salmon fillet
1 tablespoon olive oil
Salt and black pepper to taste
Fresh herbs for garnish

Preheat the oven to 400°F.
Cut the salmon into bite-sized pieces.

Arrange on a baking sheet, drizzle with olive oil, and season with salt and pepper.
Bake for 12-15 minutes or until salmon is cooked through. Garnish with fresh herbs before serving.

5. Bruschetta with Tomato and Basil

Classic Italian appetizer featuring fresh tomatoes, basil, and garlic atop crunchy toasted bread.

Ingredients:

1 loaf of whole grain baguette
2 cups cherry tomatoes
1/2 cup fresh basil
1 clove garlic
1 tablespoon olive oil
Salt and black pepper to taste

Preheat your oven to 375°F.
Slice the baguette into 1/2-inch thick slices and arrange them on a baking sheet.
Bake for 10 minutes, or until the bread is crispy and golden.
Finely chop the tomatoes, basil, and garlic, then combine them in a bowl with the olive oil. Season with salt and pepper.
Spoon the tomato mixture onto the toasted bread slices and serve.

6. Quinoa Salad Cups

Nutritious quinoa mixed with fresh veggies and lean chicken, served in crisp lettuce cups. A light and satisfying appetizer.

Ingredients:

1 cup cooked quinoa
1 cup chopped cucumber
1 cup chopped bell peppers
1 cup cooked chicken, diced

15 small lettuce leaves (like Butter or Romaine)
Salt and black pepper to taste

Combine the cooked quinoa, chopped cucumber, bell peppers, and diced chicken in a large bowl. Season with salt and pepper.
Stir the ingredients together until well-mixed.
Spoon the quinoa mixture into each lettuce cup, taking care not to overfill.
Serve the quinoa salad cups immediately, or refrigerate until ready to serve.

7. Melon and Prosciutto Skewers

Refreshing melon cubes skewered with slices of lean prosciutto – a delightful, easy-to-make appetizer.

Ingredients:

1 medium melon (like Cantaloupe or Honeydew)
15 slices of prosciutto
15 wooden skewers

Cut the melon into bite-sized cubes. Each cube should be about the same width as a slice of prosciutto.
Fold each slice of prosciutto once or twice so that it's roughly the same size as a melon cube.
Thread a melon cube and a folded slice of prosciutto onto each skewer.
Arrange the skewers on a platter and serve.

8. Baked Oatmeal Bites with Blueberries

These healthy and hearty oatmeal bites are perfect for an appetizer or a snack. The oatmeal is gentle on the stomach, and the blueberries add a touch of sweetness without triggering acid reflux.

Ingredients:

2 cups of old-fashioned oats
1 cup of blueberries
1/2 cup of honey

1/2 cup of unsweetened almond milk
1 egg

Preheat your oven to 350°F and grease a mini muffin tin.
Combine the oats, blueberries, honey, almond milk, and egg in a bowl.
Spoon the mixture into the muffin tin and bake for 15-20 minutes or until set.
Allow them to cool before serving.

9. Cucumber and Smoked Salmon Bites

Crisp cucumber rounds topped with cream cheese and smoked salmon. This recipe is a refreshing and light appetizer that's also easy on the stomach.

Ingredients:
1 cucumber
4 oz smoked salmon
4 oz cream cheese
Fresh dill for garnish

Slice the cucumber into 1/4-inch thick rounds.
Spread a small amount of cream cheese on each cucumber round.
Top with a piece of smoked salmon and garnish with dill.
Serve immediately.

10. Zucchini and Feta Fritters

Savory pan-fried fritters made from grated zucchini and crumbled feta. They're a fantastic source of nutrients, as well as being low in acid.

Ingredients:
2 medium zucchinis
1/2 cup crumbled feta cheese
1/4 cup flour
1 egg
Olive oil
Salt and pepper to taste

Grate the zucchinis and squeeze out any excess liquid.

Combine the grated zucchini, feta cheese, flour, egg, salt, and pepper in a bowl.
Heat a small amount of olive oil in a pan over medium heat.
Drop spoonfuls of the zucchini mixture into the pan and flatten with a spatula.
Cook until golden brown, about 3-4 minutes on each side.
Serve warm.

Portion control during snack time is critical to manage acid reflux symptoms successfully. The adage, "Eat until you're 80% full," is a good guidepost for you. This simple yet practical rule helps you avoid overeating, a well-known trigger for reflux symptoms. What exactly does 80% complete feel like? It's the point at which you no longer feel hungry, but you're not exactly full, either. Here, you have eaten enough to curb your hunger but haven't filled your stomach to its capacity.

Now, how can you implement portion control effectively when snacking? Here are some practical tips:

1. Pre-Portion Your Snacks: instead of snacking straight from a full-size package, divide your snacks into smaller, individual servings. For instance, don't bring the entire bag to your desk or couch if you're snacking on almonds. Measure out an ounce (roughly 23 almonds), and leave the rest in the pantry.

2. Choose Snacks Wisely: opt for snacks rich in fiber and protein, as they tend to be more filling. An excellent choice is a hard-boiled egg, a small apple with a tablespoon of almond butter, or a cup of blueberries. Even healthy snacks can lead to discomfort if you overeat at once.

3. Mindful Eating: pay attention to what you're eating and how much you're eating. Avoid distractions like TV or work while you're snacking, as it can lead to overeating. Take the time to enjoy your food, chew thoroughly, and recognize the signs when you're satisfied.

Now, let's talk about snack timing. Snacks can act as a bridge between meals, helping to prevent hunger and overeating at meal times. However, their timing plays a significant role in managing acid reflux. It's recommended to have a small snack between your main meals. Don't allow more than 3-4 hours between your meals and snacks. This pattern can help keep your blood sugar stable, curb your hunger, and prevent overeating.

Here are a few tips on snack timing.

1. Avoid Late-Night Snacking: eating late at night, especially just before bed, is a well-known trigger for acid reflux. Aim to finish eating 2-3 hours before going to bed to allow your body time to digest the food.

2. Pre-Workout Snacks: if you're planning a workout, a light snack about an hour before can give you the energy you need. However, avoid high-fat foods that can lead to discomfort during your exercise.

3. Post-Meal Snacks: if you are hungry soon after a meal, you might need to increase your meals' protein or fiber content. However, if a snack is necessary, opt for a light one, such as a piece of fruit or a small yogurt.

Everyone is unique, and what works for one person might not work for another. Listen to your body, and adjust your snacking habits to what makes you feel best. Your comfort, satiety, and well-being are the best guidelines to follow when managing your acid reflux through smart snacking.

CHAPTER 7: IRRESISTIBLE DESSERTS FOR SENSITIVE TUMMIES

When you think about managing acid reflux, one of the first things that may come to mind is having to give up desserts. After all, desserts are often high in fat, sugar, and other ingredients that can trigger reflux symptoms. But is it a myth that all desserts are off-limits? Or can you still indulge your sweet tooth without worsening your acid reflux? Let's address some of these common misconceptions and truths about desserts and acid reflux.

Misconception 1: all desserts cause acid reflux.
Truth: not all desserts are created equal, and not all will trigger acid reflux. Just like with any other food, it depends on the ingredients and the portion size. Certain ingredients like chocolate, mint, and citrus fruits are known to trigger acid reflux. However, there are many dessert recipes out there that do not use these ingredients and can be a satisfying end to a meal without causing discomfort.

Misconception 2: desserts must always be high in fat and sugar.
Truth: while traditional desserts are often high in fat and sugar, there are plenty of ways to create delicious, satisfying desserts that are lower in these components. Using natural sweeteners like bananas or applesauce, or substituting higher-fat ingredients with lower-fat alternatives, can make a significant difference in the reflux-friendliness of your dessert.

Misconception 3: I can't have chocolate if I have acid reflux.
Truth: chocolate is a known trigger for acid reflux because it contains caffeine and other stimulants that can relax the lower esophageal sphincter and increase stomach acid. However, everyone's tolerance is different. You may find that a small amount of dark chocolate doesn't worsen your symptoms. It's all about moderation and understanding your body's response.

Misconception 4: citrus fruits are a no-go in desserts.
Truth: while it's true that citrus fruits can trigger acid reflux due to their high acidity, this doesn't mean they are entirely off-limits. If you know that citrus doesn't trigger your symptoms or you can tolerate a small amount, you could experiment with including small quantities in your desserts.

Misconception 5: having dessert after dinner will always lead to nighttime acid reflux.
Truth: acid reflux can indeed be worse at night, and eating a heavy meal or dessert right before bedtime can trigger it. However, if you have dessert earlier in the evening and stay upright for at least three hours before going to bed, it can lessen the chances of nighttime reflux.

Managing acid reflux doesn't mean denying yourself all the foods you love. It's about learning what triggers your symptoms and finding satisfying alternatives when necessary. You can experiment with different ingredients and recipes to find what works best for you. Sometimes, making minor adjustments to how you prepare your dessert or the portion size can significantly affect how you feel afterward.

Treating acid reflux is a journey, not a destination. Remind yourself that it's not about deprivation but about discovering new ways to enjoy your food while feeling your best. With careful planning and a little creativity, you can still enjoy desserts and keep your acid reflux symptoms in check.

Dessert recipes using reflux-friendly ingredients

If you're a dessert lover dealing with acid reflux, you might feel as if you've been placed in a difficult position. But let's flip the script and show you how you can enjoy sweet treats that are as delightful as they are friendly to your condition. Here are some recipes that use ingredients that shouldn't trigger your acid reflux.

1. Oatmeal and Banana Cookies

Here's a treat that's easy on your tummy and your sweet tooth! These cookies are made with oats and ripe bananas, ensuring a satisfying and healthful treat. They're not only easy to make but also great for grabbing on the go.

Ingredients:

2 ripe bananas (mashed)
1 cup of oats

A pinch of salt
A sprinkle of cinnamon

Preheat your oven to 350°F. Mix all ingredients in a bowl until well combined. Drop spoonfuls onto a baking sheet lined with parchment paper. Bake for 15-20 minutes until golden brown. Cool and enjoy.

2. Almond and Pear Tart

This tart combines pears' natural sweetness with almonds' richness, creating a flavorful dessert without causing acid reflux.

Ingredients:

1 cup of almond flour
1/2 cup of unsalted butter (melted)
1/4 cup of honey
3 ripe pears (sliced)
1 tsp of vanilla extract

Preheat your oven to 350°F. Mix almond flour, melted butter, and honey to form a dough. Press this mixture into a tart pan. Arrange the pear slices on top and bake for 20-25 minutes until the crust is golden and the pears are tender. Cool before serving.

3. Coconut and Blueberry Muffins

These muffins are light, fluffy, and packed with the fresh flavor of blueberries. Coconut flour is a wonderful, fiber-rich alternative that adds a lovely hint of coconut flavor.

Ingredients:

1/2 cup of coconut flour
1/4 cup of coconut oil (melted)
4 eggs
2 tbsp of honey
1/2 cup of fresh blueberries

A pinch of salt

Preheat your oven to 350°F. Mix the coconut flour, eggs, melted coconut oil, honey, and salt until smooth. Gently fold in the blueberries. Pour into a lined muffin tray and bake for 20-25 minutes. Let them cool before enjoying.

4. Vanilla Custard

A classic dessert that is as comforting as it is delicious. Made with essential ingredients and flavored with genuine vanilla, it's a soothing choice for your acid reflux.

Ingredients:
2 cups of whole milk
4 large eggs
1/4 cup of honey
1 tsp of pure vanilla extract

Heat the milk in a saucepan over medium heat until it just starts to steam. Beat the eggs, honey, and vanilla extract in a separate bowl. Slowly pour the hot milk into the egg mixture while whisking constantly. Pour the mixture back into the saucepan and cook over low heat, stirring until the custard thickens enough to coat the back of a spoon. Do not let it boil. Strain the custard and refrigerate until chilled.

5. Almond Butter Cookies

These simple, flourless cookies are made with just a few ingredients but pack a ton of flavor. They're naturally gluten-free and a safe choice for reflux sufferers.

Ingredients:

1 cup natural almond butter
1/4 cup honey
1 large egg
1/2 teaspoon baking soda

Preheat your oven to 350°F. Mix all ingredients in a bowl until well combined. Drop spoonfuls of dough onto a parchment-lined baking sheet and flatten with a fork. Bake for 8-10 minutes until lightly golden.

6. Almond-Oat Thumbprint Cookies

These cookies are healthy, satisfying, and made with whole oats and almond flour. The thumbprint can be filled with any reflux-friendly spread of your choice.

Ingredients:

1 cup whole oats
1 cup almond flour
1/4 cup of honey
1/2 cup of natural almond butter

Instructions:
Preheat your oven to 350°F. Mix all ingredients in a bowl until well combined. Shape into small balls and place on a lined baking sheet. Make a small dent in each cookie with your thumb and fill it with a small amount of almond butter. Bake for 10-12 minutes until golden brown.

7. Gingerbread Cookies

These cookies offer the warming flavors of ginger and cinnamon, and the molasses provides a natural sweetness. They're a tasty treat that's gentle on your stomach.

Ingredients:
2 cups of almond flour
1/4 cup of molasses
2 tbsp of ground ginger
1 tsp of ground cinnamon
1/2 tsp of baking soda

Preheat your oven to 350°F. Mix all ingredients in a bowl until a dough forms. Roll out the dough and cut into shapes with cookie cutters. Bake on a parchment-lined baking sheet for 10-12 minutes until firm.

8. Maple-Cinnamon Flaxseed Pudding

This simple pudding uses flaxseeds high in fiber and omega-3 fatty acids. With a delightful hint of maple and cinnamon, it's a delicious and healthy dessert for managing acid reflux.

Ingredients:
1/4 cup of flaxseeds
1 cup of unsweetened almond milk
2 tbsp of pure maple syrup
1/2 tsp of cinnamon

Grind the flaxseeds in a food processor until they reach a coarse consistency. Mix the ground flaxseeds, almond milk, maple syrup, and cinnamon in a bowl until well combined. Refrigerate for at least 2 hours until the mixture thickens into a pudding-like consistency.

9. Vanilla Almond Meringues

These light and airy meringues are the perfect sweet treat that won't trigger your acid reflux. The combination of almond and vanilla makes for a flavorful, satisfying dessert.

Ingredients:

4 large egg whites
1/4 cup of honey
1 tsp of vanilla extract
1/2 tsp of almond extract

Preheat your oven to 225°F. Beat the egg whites in a clean, dry bowl until they hold soft peaks. Slowly add the honey, vanilla extract, and almond extract, continuing to beat until the meringues hold stiff peaks. Spoon dollops of the meringue mixture onto a baking sheet lined with parchment paper. Bake for about 1 hour or until the meringues are firm and dry to the touch. Turn off the oven and let the meringues sit inside until they are completely cool.

Fruit-based dessert recipes

While acid reflux can make enjoying desserts seem like a dream, remember that you don't have to relinquish your sweet tooth entirely. Mainly, fruit-based desserts offer an abundance of naturally sweet, satisfying flavors, as well as beneficial fiber and nutrients. But as always, the key lies in carefully selecting the right fruits that won't trigger your reflux symptoms.

Bananas, melons, pears, and apples are some fruits that are generally considered safe for those with acid reflux. They are less acidic compared to citrus fruits and tomatoes, which could lead to heartburn. However, everyone is unique, and what might work for one person may not necessarily work for you. Therefore, it's critical to identify your personal trigger foods and plan your desserts accordingly.

Now, let's explore some delightful fruit-based dessert recipes that are not only delicious but also friendly to your stomach.

1. Baked Cinnamon Bananas

This dessert not only has the natural sweetness of bananas but also the added depth of cinnamon. It's a warm, comforting dessert that's super simple to prepare.

Ingredients:
2 ripe bananas
1 tsp ground cinnamon
1 tsp honey

Preheat your oven to 350°F. Slice the bananas into rounds, arrange them in a baking dish, sprinkle with cinnamon, and drizzle with honey. Bake for 15-20 minutes until the bananas are soft and slightly caramelized.

2. Honeydew Melon Sorbet

This refreshing sorbet uses the natural sweetness of honeydew melon, making it an excellent palette cleanser or a cool treat on a hot day.

Ingredients:

4 cups of cubed honeydew melon
1/4 cup of honey
Juice of 1 lime

Blend all the ingredients in a blender until smooth. Pour the mixture into a loaf pan and freeze for at least 4 hours or overnight. When ready to serve, let it thaw for a few minutes and then scrape it with a fork to create a fluffy texture.

3. Apple-Pear Crumble

This crumble combines apples and pears, topped with a crispy oat topping for a wholesome dessert that fills your home with a lovely aroma.

Ingredients:
2 apples
2 pears
1 cup of oats
1/2 cup of almond flour
1/4 cup of melted coconut oil
2 tbsp honey
1 tsp cinnamon

Preheat your oven to 350°F. Dice the apples and pears and place them in a baking dish. Mix the oats, almond flour, coconut oil, honey, and cinnamon in a separate bowl until combined. Sprinkle the mixture over the fruits. Bake for 30-35 minutes until the topping is golden brown and the fruits are bubbly.

4. Melon and Pineapple Fruit Salad

This salad is light, refreshing, and naturally sweet. It's a fantastic palate cleanser or a light dessert.

Ingredients:

1 ripe cantaloupe
1 ripe pineapple
juice of 1 lime

Dice the melon and pineapple and place them in a large bowl. Squeeze the lime juice over the fruit and gently toss to combine. Chill in the refrigerator before serving.

5. Poached Pears in Cinnamon Syrup

Poached pears are a classic dessert. The pears are soft and infused with a sweet cinnamon syrup, making for a warm and comforting dish.

Ingredients:
4 ripe pears
2 cups water
1/2 cup honey
1 cinnamon stick

Peel the pears, leaving the stem intact. In a large pot, bring the water, honey, and cinnamon stick to a simmer. Add the pears, cover, and simmer for 20-25 minutes, until the pears are tender. Serve warm.

6. Melon Balls with Mint

This refreshing dessert combines the coolness of melon with the zing of mint for a light and fresh palate cleanser.

Ingredients:

1 ripe cantaloupe
1 ripe honeydew melon
fresh mint leaves
1 tbsp honey

Scoop out the melons using a melon baller and place them in a large bowl. Chop a handful of mint leaves and sprinkle them over the melon. Drizzle with honey and gently toss to combine. Chill in the refrigerator before serving.

7. Strawberry Banana Ice Cream

This two-ingredient "ice cream" uses only fruit to create a delightful and refreshing dessert that won't cause acid reflux.

Ingredients:

2 ripe bananas
1 cup strawberries

Peel and slice the bananas, then freeze until solid. Remove from the freezer and blend with the strawberries in a food processor until smooth. You can serve it immediately or freeze it for later use.

8. Roasted Berries with Oat Topping

Roasting brings out the natural sweetness in berries, while an oat topping adds a comforting, crumble-like texture.

Ingredients:

2 cups mixed berries (such as blueberries and strawberries)
1 cup oats
2 tbsp coconut oil
2 tbsp honey

Preheat the oven to 350°F. Spread the berries in a baking dish. Mix the oats, coconut oil, and honey, then sprinkle over the berries. Bake for 20-25 minutes until the berries are bubbling and the oats are golden.

9. Pineapple Ginger Sorbet

This refreshing sorbet combines the sweetness of pineapple with a touch of invigorating ginger. An excellent palette cleanser that is also friendly to your reflux symptoms.

Ingredients:
1 ripe pineapple
1 tbsp fresh ginger
Juice of 1 lime

Peel and chop the pineapple, then freeze the chunks until solid. Peel and grate the ginger. Once the pineapple is frozen, blend it in a food processor with the ginger and lime juice until smooth. You can serve this immediately, or freeze it for a firmer texture.

10. Blueberry Oat Bars

A delightful, wholesome dessert filled with the natural sweetness of blueberries. These oat bars are easy to make and gentle on your stomach.

Ingredients:

1 cup rolled oats
1/2 cup almond flour
2 tbsp honey
3 tbsp coconut oil
1 cup fresh blueberries

Preheat your oven to 350°F. Combine the oats, almond flour, honey, and coconut oil in a bowl. Press half of this mixture into a greased baking dish. Spread the blueberries over it, then sprinkle the remaining oat mixture on top. Bake for 20-25 minutes, or until the top is golden.

While diving into the world of reflux-friendly desserts, it's important to remember one fundamental principle: moderation. Even though these desserts are designed to be gentler on your stomach, consuming large amounts in one sitting can still lead to discomfort and trigger acid reflux symptoms. Moderation is the balance between deprivation and overindulgence, and it plays a vital role in managing your acid reflux while allowing you to enjoy the sweet things in life.

Think of it this way, even when you're staying hydrated with water, drinking too much at once can make you feel uncomfortable. The same principle applies to eating, especially when it comes to desserts. Desserts, by their nature, are typically rich and sweet, qualities that could potentially stimulate acid production in the stomach when consumed in large quantities.

Keeping portion sizes reasonable helps to maintain this balance. So, instead of reaching for a second slice of that delectable almond honey cake or a heaping bowl of banana oatmeal cookies, opt for a modest portion. One slice of cake, or one or two cookies, is often enough to satisfy your sweet tooth without overwhelming your stomach. And remember, it's not just about the quantity of the food you consume, but also the pace. Eating slowly and mindfully allows your body ample time to process food, leading to better digestion and absorption.

Now that we've established the significance of moderation, here are some tips for enjoying desserts while keeping acid reflux symptoms at bay:

Balance your meal: If you plan on having a dessert, balance your meal accordingly. If you know you're going to indulge in a sweet treat, make sure your main meal is lighter and contains plenty of vegetables.

Consider your personal triggers: While these recipes are designed to be reflux-friendly, everyone's body reacts differently. If you know that a specific ingredient triggers your acid reflux, swap it for something else that you can tolerate better.

Hydrate: Staying well-hydrated can help dilute stomach acid and keep your digestive system running smoothly. Try to drink a glass of water before and after your dessert.

Space out your dessert: Instead of having dessert right after dinner, give your body some time to digest the main meal first. This can help prevent overfilling your stomach and triggering acid reflux.

Choose wisely: Opt for desserts that are less fatty and less sugary. The reflux-friendly dessert recipes shared earlier in this guide are a great place to start!

By keeping these points in mind, you can maintain the balance that allows you to manage your acid reflux while still indulging in the occasional dessert. After all, treating yourself shouldn't come at the cost of your comfort. Enjoying dessert in moderation allows you to maintain your health without giving up the joys of a sweet ending to your meal.

CHAPTER 8: 28-DAY MEAL PLAN

On the road to managing your acid reflux, one tool that can provide immense support is a structured meal plan. A well-designed meal plan offers numerous benefits, many of which go beyond just easing acid reflux symptoms.

1. Easier to Avoid Trigger Foods: when you follow a meal plan, you can ensure that you're consistently avoiding foods that trigger your acid reflux symptoms. You'll have a clear idea of what you'll be eating for each meal and snack, making it easier to steer clear of those foods and ingredients that do more harm than good.

2. Balanced Nutrition: a meal plan can help you get all the nutrients your body needs to function optimally. By planning your meals, you can incorporate various foods that provide a wide range of nutrients, ensuring a balanced diet.

3. Weight Management: a meal plan can be incredibly beneficial if weight loss or maintenance is part of your health goals. Planning your meals allows you to control portion sizes and nutrient intake, supporting healthy weight management, which can help reduce acid reflux symptoms.

4. Reduces Stress: deciding what to eat can be a source of stress, especially when dealing with dietary restrictions like those required for managing acid reflux. A meal plan removes the daily guesswork, reducing stress and making it easier for you to stick to your reflux-friendly diet.

5. Promotes Consistent Eating Habits: a structured meal plan can help regularize your eating times, which is beneficial for managing acid reflux. Regular meals can prevent overeating and avoid long periods of an empty stomach, both of which can trigger acid reflux symptoms.

6. Saves Time and Money: once you have your meal plan, grocery shopping becomes more efficient because you know exactly what you need. This saves you time and money, reducing the likelihood of impulse purchases.

7. Encourages Variety: a meal plan can help you avoid getting stuck in a food rut and repeatedly eating the same meals. By planning, you can incorporate various foods into your diet, making it more enjoyable and sustainable.

8. Enhances Digestive Health: regular, balanced meals and snacks can improve your overall digestive health. A healthy digestive system is key in managing acid reflux symptoms.

While the idea of meal planning might seem daunting at first, remember that it doesn't have to be perfect. Start with a few days at a time, then gradually work up to planning a week or more. The most important thing is to create a plan that works for you - one that makes your life easier, your body healthier, and your meals more enjoyable.

Through it all, keep in mind that you're not alone in this journey. As you've discovered from the previous sections, you can enjoy plenty of delicious, varied, and satisfying foods, even while managing acid reflux. With some planning and preparation, you can nourish your body, soothe your symptoms, and savor the joy of eating.

28-Day Meal Plan

The following is a comprehensive 28-day meal plan specially designed to help you manage your acid reflux symptoms while also ensuring you consume various tasty and nutritious meals. This plan includes breakfast, lunch, dinner, and two daily snack options.

Week 1

Day 1:

- **Breakfast:** Almond Banana Smoothie
- **Mid-Morning Snack:** Baked Banana Chips
- **Lunch:** Chicken Avocado Salad with Lemon
  Vinaigrette
- **Afternoon Snack:** Carrot and Cucumber Sticks
  with Hummus

- **Dinner:** Quinoa Primavera
- **Dessert:** Oatmeal and Banana Cookies

Day 2:

- **Breakfast:** Classic Oatmeal with a Twist
- **Mid-Morning Snack:** Greek Yogurt with a drizzle of Honey
- **Lunch:** Baked Salmon with Dill and Lemon, served with a side of Steamed Green Beans
- **Afternoon Snack:** Apple Almond Delight
- **Dinner:** Chicken and Vegetable Stir-fry
- **Dessert:** Almond and Pear Tart

Day 3:

- **Breakfast:** Poached Eggs with Avocado
- **Mid-Morning Snack:** Rice Cake with Almond Butter
- **Lunch:** Ginger Carrot Soup
- **Afternoon Snack:** Turkey Roll-ups
- **Dinner:** Baked Cod with Lemon and Herbs, served with a side of Quinoa Salad
- **Dessert:** Melon and Mint Sorbet

Day 4:

- **Breakfast:** Berry Oatmeal Smoothie
- **Mid-Morning Snack:** Rice Cake and Avocado
- **Lunch:** Greek Salad with Grilled Chicken
- **Afternoon Snack:** Chia Pudding
- **Dinner:** Chicken and Brown Rice Casserole
- **Dessert:** Coconut and Blueberry Muffins

Day 5:

- **Breakfast:** Savory Oatmeal with Avocado

- **Mid-Morning Snack:** Carrot and Cucumber Sticks with Hummus
- **Lunch:** Creamy Zucchini Soup
- **Afternoon Snack:** Baked Zucchini Chips
- **Dinner:** Oven-Roasted Turkey Breast with a side of Baked Sweet Potato
- **Dessert:** Berry and Banana Smoothie

Day 6:

- **Breakfast:** Hard-Boiled Eggs with Quinoa Salad
- **Mid-Morning Snack:** Roasted Chickpeas
- **Lunch:** Chickpea and Feta Salad with Mint Yogurt Dressing
- **Afternoon Snack:** Pumpkin Seed & Dried Fruit Mix
- **Dinner:** Baked Cod with Lemon and Herbs, served with a side of Quinoa Salad
- **Dessert:** Vanilla Custard

Day 7:

- **Breakfast:** Pumpkin Spice Oatmeal
- **Mid-Morning Snack:** Almond Butter Rice Cakes
- **Lunch:** Grilled Turkey Breast with a side of Roasted Brussels Sprouts
- **Afternoon Snack:** Hummus and Veggie Sticks
- **Dinner:** Shrimp and Farro Paella
- **Dessert:** Apple and Pear Crumble

Week 2

Day 8:

- **Breakfast:** Ginger Pear Smoothie
- **Mid-Morning Snack:** Carrot and Cucumber Sticks with Hummus
- **Lunch:** Oven-Roasted Turkey Breast with a side of

Baked Sweet Potato
- **Afternoon Snack:** Bruschetta with Tomato and Basil
- **Dinner:** Baked Salmon with Quinoa and Broccoli
- **Dessert:** Almond Butter Cookies

Day 9:

- **Breakfast:** Scrambled Eggs with Fresh Herbs
- **Mid-Morning Snack:** Baked Banana Chips
- **Lunch:** Chicken and Rice Soup
- **Afternoon Snack:** Carrot and Cucumber Sticks with Hummus
- **Dinner:** Grilled Chicken with Quinoa and Steamed Veggies
- **Dessert:** Berry and Banana Smoothie

Day 10:

- **Breakfast:** Apple Cinnamon Oatmeal
- **Mid-Morning Snack:** Greek Yogurt with a drizzle of Honey
- **Lunch:** Broccoli and Cauliflower Salad with Tahini Dressing
- **Afternoon Snack:** Melon and Prosciutto Skewers
- **Dinner:** Chicken and Vegetable Stir-fry
- **Dessert:** Poached Pears in Cinnamon Syrup

Day 11:

- **Breakfast:** Green Goddess Smoothie
- **Mid-Morning Snack:** Rice Cake with Almond Butter
- **Lunch:** Egg Salad Wrap
- **Afternoon Snack:** Apple Almond Delight
- **Dinner:** Baked Cod with Lemon and Herbs, served with a side of Quinoa Salad
- **Dessert:** Coconut and Blueberry Muffins

Day 12:

- **Breakfast:** Veggie Omelet
- **Mid-Morning Snack:** Rice Cake and Avocado
- **Lunch:** Grilled Chicken Salad with Lettuce and Cucumbers
- **Afternoon Snack:** Roasted Chickpeas
- **Dinner:** Baked Salmon with Quinoa and Roasted Asparagus
- **Dessert:** Melon and Pineapple Fruit Salad

Day 13:

- **Breakfast:** Oatmeal with Almond Butter and Banana
- **Mid-Morning Snack:** Carrot and Cucumber Sticks with Hummus
- **Lunch:** Hummus & Veggie Wrap
- **Afternoon Snack:** Chia Pudding
- **Dinner:** Oven-Roasted Turkey Breast with a side of Baked Sweet Potato
- **Dessert:** Melon and Mint Sorbet

Day 14:

- **Breakfast:** Chia Seed Tropical Smoothie
- **Mid-Morning Snack:** Oatmeal Raisin Cookies
- **Lunch:** Grilled Salmon with Lemon and Dill, served with a side of Steamed Green Beans
- **Afternoon Snack:** Baked Zucchini Chips
- **Dinner:** Baked Tofu with Veggies
- **Dessert:** Honeydew Melon Sorbet

Week 3

Day 15:

- **Breakfast:** Avocado and Egg White Scramble
- **Mid-Morning Snack:** Pumpkin Seed & Dried Fruit Mix
- **Lunch:** Tuna and White Bean Salad with Dill Dressing
- **Afternoon Snack:** Carrot and Cucumber Sticks with Hummus
- **Dinner:** Grilled Shrimp Skewers with a side of Steamed Vegetables
- **Dessert:** Gingerbread Cookies

Day 16:

- **Breakfast:** Pear and Ginger Oatmeal
- **Mid-Morning Snack:** Baked Banana Chips
- **Lunch:** Cauliflower and Garlic Soup
- **Afternoon Snack:** Rice Cake with Avocado Spread
- **Dinner:** Baked Cod with Lemon and Herbs, served with a side of Quinoa Salad
- **Dessert:** Baked Cinnamon Bananas

Day 17:

- **Breakfast:** Vanilla Cinnamon Smoothie
- **Mid-Morning Snack:** Carrot and Cucumber Sticks with Hummus
- **Lunch:** Grilled Salmon with Lemon and Dill, served with a side of Steamed Green Beans
- **Afternoon Snack:** Greek Yogurt with a drizzle of Honey
- **Dinner:** Oven-Roasted Turkey Breast with a side of Baked Sweet Potato
- **Dessert:** Apple and Pear Crumble

Day 18:

- **Breakfast:** Baked Eggs with Asparagus
- **Mid-Morning Snack:** Apple Almond Delight
- **Lunch:** Grilled Chicken Salad with Lettuce and Cucumbers
- **Afternoon Snack:** Turkey Roll-ups
- **Dinner:** Quinoa-Stuffed Bell Peppers
- **Dessert:** Vanilla Almond Meringues

Day 19:

- **Breakfast:** Tropical Oatmeal
- **Mid-Morning Snack:** Greek Yogurt with a drizzle of Honey
- **Lunch:** Greek Salad with Grilled Chicken
- **Afternoon Snack:** Rice Cake and Avocado
- **Dinner:** Grilled Shrimp Skewers with a side of Steamed Vegetables
- **Dessert:** Maple-Cinnamon Flaxseed Pudding

Day 20:

- **Breakfast:** Blueberry Apple Smoothie
- **Mid-Morning Snack:** Chia Pudding
- **Lunch:** Grilled Veggie and Quinoa Salad with Basil Vinaigrette
- **Afternoon Snack:** Carrot and Cucumber Sticks with Hummus
- **Dinner:** Chicken and Vegetable Stir-fry
- **Dessert:** Oat and Almond Cookies

Day 21:

- **Breakfast:** Egg, Tomato, and Basil Open-Face Sandwich
- **Mid-Morning Snack:** Oatmeal Raisin Cookies
- **Lunch:** Barley and Mushroom Soup
- **Afternoon Snack:** Baked Zucchini Chips

- **Dinner:** Turkey and Brown Rice Stuffed Peppers
- **Dessert:** Berry and Banana Smoothie

Week 4

Day 22:

- **Breakfast:** Oatmeal with Raisins and Cinnamon
- **Mid-Morning Snack:** Greek Yogurt with a drizzle of Honey
- **Lunch:** Grilled Chicken & Avocado Wrap
- **Afternoon Snack:** Baked Banana Chips
- **Dinner:** Baked Cod with Lemon and Herbs, served with a side of Quinoa Salad
- **Dessert:** Vanilla Almond Meringues

Day 23:

- **Breakfast:** Mango Avocado Smoothie
- **Mid-Morning Snack:** Carrot and Cucumber Sticks with Hummus
- **Lunch:** Grilled Salmon with Lemon and Dill, served with a side of Steamed Green Beans
- **Afternoon Snack:** Greek Yogurt with a drizzle of Honey
- **Dinner:** Turkey Chili with Sweet Potato
- **Dessert:** Baked Pears with Cinnamon and Almonds

Day 24:

- **Breakfast:** Mediterranean Egg Muffins
- **Mid-Morning Snack:** Apple Almond Delight
- **Lunch:** Greek-Style Wrap
- **Afternoon Snack:** Rice Cake and Avocado
- **Dinner:** Quinoa-Stuffed Bell Peppers
- **Dessert:** Baked Cinnamon Bananas

Day 25:

- **Breakfast:** Oatmeal with Raisins and Cinnamon
- **Mid-Morning Snack:** Rice Cake with Almond Butter
- **Lunch:** Spinach and White Bean Soup
- **Afternoon Snack:** Greek Yogurt with a drizzle of Honey
- **Dinner:** Oven-Roasted Turkey Breast with a side of Baked Sweet Potato
- **Dessert:** Coconut and Blueberry Muffins

Day 26:

- **Breakfast:** Quinoa and Veggie Scramble
- **Mid-Morning Snack:** Oatmeal Raisin Cookies
- **Lunch:** Grilled Turkey Breast with a side of Roasted Brussels Sprouts
- **Afternoon Snack:** Rice Cake with Avocado Spread
- **Dinner:** Baked Cod with Lemon and Herbs, served with a side of Quinoa Salad
- **Dessert:** Honeydew Melon Sorbet

Day 27:

- **Breakfast:** Vanilla Cinnamon Smoothie
- **Mid-Morning Snack:** Baked Zucchini Chips
- **Lunch:** Tofu & Veggie Wrap
- **Afternoon Snack:** Greek Yogurt with a drizzle of Honey
- **Dinner:** Herb-Roasted Chicken and Brussels Sprouts
- **Dessert:** Almond Butter Cookies

Day 28:

- **Breakfast:** Cherry Almond Oatmeal
- **Mid-Morning Snack:** Rice Cake with Almond

Butter
- **Lunch:** Grilled Salmon with Lemon and Dill,
  served with a side of Steamed Green Beans
- **Afternoon Snack:** Baked Banana Chips
- **Dinner:** Baked Tilapia with Couscous and
  Steamed Zucchini
- **Dessert:** Melon and Pineapple Fruit Salad

And there you have it, a comprehensive 28-day meal plan to manage your acid reflux while ensuring you enjoy a variety of tasty and nutritious meals. Remember to keep up with good hydration, and feel free to adjust the portions and timings to suit your specific needs and lifestyle. This plan is intended to control your acid reflux symptoms and promote a balanced and healthful diet. Enjoy!

You've embarked on this path, the 28-day meal plan designed to manage acid reflux symptoms. You've seen the potential for tasty and nutritious meals that still keep those symptoms at bay. But you're an individual, and there's no one-size-fits-all solution to diet. Your body is unique, your preferences are your own, and your daily routines vary. Recognizing this, adjusting the meal plan to cater to your individual needs and preferences is essential.

Firstly, consider portion sizes. The meal plan provides suggestions for meals and snacks throughout the day. If you find that the portion sizes are too large or too small, feel free to adjust them. Listen to your body. If a smaller breakfast and a larger lunch work better for you, go for it. If you prefer to have two smaller snacks instead of one larger snack between meals, that's fine too. The key is to avoid overeating and maintain a balanced intake of nutrients throughout the day.

Next, think about the timing of your meals. Some people might prefer six smaller meals, while others might only need three. What's critical is to avoid eating 2-3 hours before bedtime to lessen the likelihood of nighttime reflux. If you're an early riser, you might have breakfast earlier and need a mid-morning snack. If you're a night owl, you might have dinner later but remember to give your body time to digest before sleeping.

Now, let's talk about your food preferences. Not everyone enjoys all foods, and that's perfectly okay. If there's a vegetable or protein in the meal plan that you don't want, feel free to substitute it. The goal is to replace it with something of similar nutritional value that is also low in acid. For example, if you don't like salmon, you can substitute it with another lean protein like turkey.

On that note, variety is not just the spice of life, but it's also key to a balanced diet. Eating a range of foods ensures you get a mix of different nutrients. If you find you're eating the same fruit or vegetable often, try mixing it up. Maybe swap out the blueberries in your morning oatmeal for some raspberries, or try a new vegetable in your stir-fry.

You know your body best. Pay attention to how you feel after eating certain foods. While the meal plan avoids common trigger foods, you might discover that other foods trigger your symptoms. If that's the case, limit or avoid these foods.

This meal plan is a tool for you. It's flexible and meant to serve you, not vice versa. The ultimate goal is to manage your symptoms, enjoy what you're eating, and promote overall health. So go ahead, make adjustments, and find what works best for you. Here's to your health and enjoying food, free from the discomfort of acid reflux!

Managing acid reflux symptoms while maintaining a vibrant and satisfying diet might seem like a challenging task. However, with the right approach and some savvy meal preparation techniques, you'll find that adhering to the meal plan becomes simpler and even more enjoyable. Here are some key strategies to make following the meal plan easier.

Firstly, don't underestimate the power of planning. At the start of each week, take a moment to look over the meal plan. Familiarize yourself with the recipes, noting any ingredients you need to purchase or steps that require more time. By doing this, you'll avoid the last-minute stress of not having what you need, allowing your meal preparation to be a calm and controlled process.

Next, consider shopping strategically. Grocery shopping can be an exciting journey of discovering new foods and flavors that are both delicious and acid-reflux-friendly. Make a list based on the meal plan and stick to it. This not only ensures you have everything you need for the week, but it also avoids impulse buys of items that might trigger your acid reflux.

Batch cooking can be a great time-saver. Whenever possible, prepare foods in larger quantities, which can then be portioned and stored for later use. For instance, consider cooking extra if a recipe calls for cooked quinoa. It stores well in the fridge and can be quickly added to meals or used as a base for another recipe.

A well-stocked pantry is a great asset. Keep it filled with reflux-friendly staples like whole grains, lean proteins, and low-acid fruits and veggies. These readily available ingredients make it easier to stick to the plan and ensure you always have quick, healthy meal options.

Proper storage is another factor that can make meal prep a breeze. When you make meals or ingredients in advance, store them in clear, airtight containers. This not only extends their shelf life but also lets you see what's available at a glance. Consider labeling containers with the date of preparation to keep track of freshness.

Next, make use of time-saving tools. A slow cooker can be a fantastic investment. It allows you to prepare your meal in the morning and then come home to a ready dinner. A blender is great for smoothies and sauces, while a good quality knife set makes chopping veggies and lean proteins quicker and safer.

Don't forget to consider the joy of leftovers. Cooking once and eating twice (or more) is a great time saver. Many of our dinner recipes can make a delicious lunch the next day. For example, the grilled chicken from dinner can be used in a salad or wrap for lunch.

Try to make meal prep a part of your routine. Maybe Sunday afternoons are a good time for you to prepare meals for the week, or perhaps an hour in the evening works best. Find a time that suits your schedule and make it a habit.

Meal prep is not a one-size-fits-all concept. Everyone has different schedules, dietary preferences, and cooking skills. The goal is to make the process efficient, enjoyable, and, most importantly, tailored to you. This way, adhering to the meal plan won't just be manageable; it'll be a part of your lifestyle, a positive and sustainable change.

CONCLUSION

Your path through understanding and managing acid reflux has provided you with abundant knowledge. The knowledge that your dietary choices play an instrumental role in managing GERD (Gastroesophageal Reflux Disease) and LPR (Laryngopharyngeal Reflux) is at the very core of that understanding. As we wrap up, let's revisit the key insights from each segment to cement your knowledge and recall.

From the first point, you grasped the fundamentals of acid reflux - what causes it, common symptoms, and the long-term health implications if left unmanaged. You understood that lifestyle modifications, particularly dietary changes, play a significant role in managing this condition, setting the stage for the following points.

In exploring breakfast ideas, you learned that starting the day right is crucial. The importance of a protein-rich breakfast, coupled with low-acid fruits and whole grains, was highlighted. You also gained a repertoire of delightful, reflux-friendly recipes like the 'Protein-packed Scramble' and the 'Almond Butter and Banana Toast' to start your mornings with zest and flavor.

While discussing lunches, the need to include lean proteins, low-fat dairy products, and a variety of vegetables in your mid-day meals was stressed. Recipes like the 'Grilled Chicken Salad' and 'Quinoa Veggie Stir-fry' provided you with nourishing and appetizing options for satisfying lunches.

The dinner discourse illuminated the importance of light, early dinners in acid reflux management. You were encouraged to incorporate lean meats, fish, whole grains, and a spectrum of vegetables into your evening meals. Recipes like 'Baked Salmon with Dill and Lemon' and 'Stuffed Bell Peppers' served to inspire delightful, healthy dinner experiences.

The snacks and appetizers discussion broke down the critical role of these small bites in managing acid reflux. You learned about portion control, the importance of timing, and several recipe ideas for tasty and beneficial snacks. Various appetizers like 'Hummus with Veggie Sticks' and 'Melon and

Prosciutto Skewers' were introduced to provide wholesome, enjoyable choices for gatherings or parties.

In tackling desserts, you confronted the common misconceptions about desserts triggering acid reflux. We emphasized moderation and careful ingredient selection. You've been armed with several delectable, reflux-friendly dessert recipes like the 'Cinnamon Ginger Cookies' and 'Apple Crumble.'

You discovered the benefits of a structured 28-day meal plan in managing acid reflux. Packed with diverse, nutritious meals, the program was designed to ease your transition into this new dietary lifestyle. You also learned how to adjust the plan to your preferences and gained tips for efficient meal prep.

Throughout this process, you've acquired not just recipes but a philosophy of eating that respects and works with your body. Every individual's response to food can differ. Listen to your body, notice which foods cause discomfort, and adjust your diet accordingly. This self-awareness, coupled with the knowledge you've gained, equips you to manage acid reflux effectively. You've taken control of your health and, in doing so, significantly improved your quality of life.

As we stand at this journey's culmination, let's look back at one of the essential messages you've embraced: you can truly enjoy your food while managing acid reflux. It's not an either-or situation. Your life with food is not destined to be a struggle, filled with dread over potential flare-ups of heartburn or throat discomfort. Instead, it's become a dance, a careful yet joyful ballet of delicious and nutritious choices that satisfy your palate and protect your health.

Food, you've learned, doesn't just sustain us—it's a source of joy, a cornerstone of our social interactions, a cultural touchstone, and a vital part of your self-care. It's something to be savored and enjoyed, not feared. You've come to understand that a life managing GERD or LPR is not a life devoid of gastronomic delight.

In fact, in many ways, it's quite the opposite. Armed with your new knowledge, you've unlocked a world of culinary possibilities, all tailored to your needs. You've embraced meals like the 'Baked Salmon with Dill' and snacks like

'Veggie Sticks with Hummus.' You've learned that desserts can be both delicious and comfortable, as you've indulged in delights like 'Pumpkin Pudding.' Each bite has been taken with the confidence and assurance that you're nourishing your body and taking control of your health.

And as you take that control, you're inspired to savor every bite. Enjoy not just the taste of your food but the feeling of eating on your terms, of knowing that you're not just reacting to your condition but actively managing it. It's a form of culinary empowerment—every meal, snack, and dessert is a testament to your commitment to your well-being, and every bite celebrates that commitment.

However, this is not the end of your path. Your road to better digestive health is ongoing, filled with more meals to enjoy, more recipes to try, and more experiences to savor. The tools you've gathered—your understanding of acid reflux, your knowledge of reflux-friendly foods, your mastery of portion control and meal timing, and your 28-day meal plan—are your guides as you move forward.

Remember, improvement doesn't mean perfection. There may be days when managing your symptoms feels more challenging than others. That's okay. These moments do not define your journey; your resilience and dedication to prioritizing your health do. The aim is not to never experience acid reflux again—it's to live a life where acid reflux doesn't dictate your choices but instead informs them.

So, embrace the comfort that comes with control, savor every bite of your meals with confidence, and boldly move forward toward better digestive health. You're not just eating to live—you're eating to thrive, enjoy, and experience. And in doing so, you're not just managing acid reflux—you're living a life full of flavor, joy, and well-being. Keep exploring, savoring, and, most importantly, enjoying your way toward better health.

You've made it. As you close this guide, you don't finish a mere book; you finalize an essential chapter of your journey toward managing and controlling your acid reflux. It's an empowering step, a choice that puts you in the driver's seat. It's your health, your body, and now, your command over it. That's the power you've harnessed in following a reflux-friendly diet. You have the reins now, and I can't wait to see where this path takes you.

Throughout this guide, you've learned that living with acid reflux doesn't mean you have to compromise on your love for food or the enjoyment of savoring a delicious meal. You've discovered you can still have a rich, varied diet and enjoy the flavors you love without triggering symptoms. And most importantly, you've seen firsthand that a reflux-friendly diet is effective. You've seen changes, big and small, in the way you feel and the way you approach food. The most beautiful thing is to feel the difference and know that you have made it.

I know that managing your acid reflux has probably not been easy. But remember, every small change you've made, every new habit you've formed, and every new recipe you've tried is a testament to your courage, determination, and resilience. It's about more than managing symptoms; it's about reclaiming your life and freedom to enjoy food. And that's an achievement worth celebrating.

As you move forward, I want you to know that the effectiveness of a reflux-friendly diet doesn't end when you close this guide. It's not a one-time remedy but a lifestyle change, a lifelong journey towards better health. So, keep exploring, keep learning, and keep savoring every bite. Remember, you've got this. You're not just surviving; you're thriving, all while enjoying your favorite foods.

Before we part ways, I want to thank you for choosing this guide. Being a part of your path has been an honor and a privilege. Your trust and your commitment to taking charge of your health have been the driving force behind this guide. I hope it has provided you with valuable insights, practical guidance, and plenty of tasty recipes to keep you satisfied and your symptoms at bay.

As we say goodbye, I leave you with a heartfelt thank you and a message of positivity. A reflux-friendly diet is more than a tool to manage your acid reflux; it's a catalyst for a healthier, happier life. Living your life on your terms's the key to enjoying food without fear. So, keep moving forward, making those delicious meals, and listening to your body.

Thank you for choosing this guide and making the brave decision to take control of your health. You have the tools, the knowledge, and the power to manage your acid reflux effectively. Here's to you and to the countless delightful, reflux-friendly meals to come. Keep shining, persevering, and believing in the power of a well-managed diet. You've got this.

If you think you enjoyed this book and it helped you, I kindly ask you to take a few moments to leave a short review on Amazon.

Thank you, Sara Creighton

Made in United States
North Haven, CT
15 March 2024

50038093R00070